AiR

The Poetry of Art

Summer Hill Seven

Author of Autobiography of Ray-Ray
& Other Ancient Ideas Like Hip-Hop

authorHOUSE

AuthorHouse™
1663 Liberty Drive
Bloomington, IN 47403
www.authorhouse.com
Phone: 833-262-8899

© 2024 Raymond Akbar, LLC dba Summer Hill Seven. All rights reserved.

No part of this book may be reproduced, stored in a retrieval system, or transmitted by any means without the written permission of the author.

Published by AuthorHouse 11/18/2024

ISBN: 979-8-8230-3111-0 (sc)
ISBN: 979-8-8230-3112-7 (hc)
ISBN: 979-8-8230-3110-3 (e)

Cover design and illustrated by:
Sharmin Islam Mannan

Library of Congress Control Number: 2024916660

Front photograph of the author by Che Ayende

Rear photograph on the dust jacket of the author by Che Ayende

The front photograph on the dust jacket of the author is a selfie.

Print information available on the last page.

Any people depicted in stock imagery provided by Getty Images are models, and such images are being used for illustrative purposes only. Certain stock imagery © Getty Images.

This book is printed on acid-free paper.

Because of the dynamic nature of the Internet, any web addresses or links contained in this book may have changed since publication and may no longer be valid. The views expressed in this work are solely those of the author and do not necessarily reflect the views of the publisher, and the publisher hereby disclaims any responsibility for them.

AiR

Dedication:

To Nina M., Sandy R., Jewel W., Joann B., Leslie R., Steve T., Deena B., Anthony Z., Gene L., Laurence H., Adrian H., Andrew W., Walter D., and many others for sharing the ancient mystery of accessing the eternal.

CONTENTS

Cora's Introduction ❁6

Chapter 1: AiR ❁13
Essalogue 1: Dream ❁14
    Movement 1 ❁18
Essalogue 2: Investment ❁47
    Movement 2 ❁53
Essalogue 3: Association ❁64
    Essalogue within an Essalogue:
    Name Unborn ❁76

Chapter 2: The Poetry ❁93
Essalogue 4: Technique ❁94
    Movement 3 ❁98
Essalogue 5: Action and Movement
    yield Autonomy ❁134
Essalogue 6: Personal Victories ❁145

Chapter 3: Of Art ❁150
Essalogue 7: Artistry ❁151

Testament ❁167

Cora's Conclusion ❁170

Acknowledgements ❁173

Annotated Bibliography ❁177

About Poemedy ❁182

About the Author ❁184

"When I was younger I could remember everything whether it happened or not."

- Autobiography of Mark Twain

Cora is my name. I speak to you from beyond the grave because the reports of my death have been greatly exaggerated. I am a mother. I am a grandmother and beyond. I am the great grandmother of the man on the cover of this book. I raised his mother, Jimmy, as if she was my own child. Jimmy was, in fact, my grandbaby. You will hear from her because she speaks loudest through the man on the cover of this book, the author and her baby boy. The baby on the cover is Jimmy's grandbaby.

AIR is all I am now. I am air and quantum bits of carbon, hydrogen, oxygen, nitrogen, and phosphorus. Yet, I am mostly air.

What about you?

Jimmy came to be raised by me when my daughter, Millie, left her in my mailbox on a country road in Florence, Alabama on February 24, 1935. Jimmy is Millie's only child, at least the only one I ever found alive.

This book intends to answer only one question. The one question is simply how do you become a better artist, creator and more specifically, a better actor. My great-grandson is an artist. He started this book alone and we will finish it together. The artist must know or invent an origin story from which to create. If you are an artist and you have no knowledge of your origin nor any story about your origin then you have yet to create your most vital creation.

Admittedly, the answer to the question of how to become a better artist is often enigmatical. The answer is like air, ubiquitous and yet mysterious. The answer to all of life's questions are more easily answered once life is completed. The answer is already in you and our role is to fuel your urge for greatness. Be air with me. Be an Artist-in-Residence (AiR) with my great-grandson.

Air. Invisible. Circulating. Ubiquitous. Unavoidable. Everywhere all at once. That I am air is my reality; my personal experience of reality; my perspective; my justification for continued participation in the human experiment; and my great-grandson's philosophical position. Pragmatically speaking it is also an acronym for a long sought-after station in the life of my great-grandson namely, an Artist-in-Residence.

This is a story about being air while being an Artist-in-Residence with Stockton University. This is a story about being an actor. This is a story about being an artist. This is a story about being an heir to a particular tradition. This is also a story about being an Artist-in-Residence at my great-grandson's alma Mater, Stockton.

This is a story about being invisible. In fact, I am so invisible that even when examined under a microscope the evidence of my existence is unseeable. The visible evidence of my continued existence is the poetry, poemedy and philosophy in these seven essalogues presented in three chapters.

You will learn how to live more abundantly onstage and off. You will learn practices and how to develop your own practices to give you abundance in your work and your life. My great-grandson practices breathing air whenever he rehearses. When he performs, he allows the air to breathe him into it. He will urge you to experiment with your practices and learn from his triumphs and disasters.

When he performs he doesn't breathe the way he practiced in rehearsal. As saxophonist Sonny Rollins says so succinctly, "you can't think and play at the same time." When he performs he wants the air to breathe him. Most actors are merely breathing air. Some even stop breathing while performing.

When the air breathes you then you have direct access to the eternal and infinite source that creates worlds. This conversation is about accessing the eternal. This is how I came to be in this conversation because the way that my great-grandson has learned to breathe has given him access to an infinite and eternal source of knowledge, wisdom and understanding. You are composed of air and quantum bits of eternal matter. You consist of the same stuff as the entire universe.

You are the audience and the intended recipient for this simple yet sincere message. Whether your stars are ruled by earth, water, fire or air you are inevitably connected to all four elements. As we investigate the element of air together we will grow in our collective self awareness. Our conversation will become more intentional. Our practices will be influenced by our identity. My identity, like air, consists of many elements, including being a Negro woman artist. You will notice an occasional use of a wide variety of terms to describe my identity, including Negro, Cherokee, Irish, woman, etc., which were taught to us while our body was visible. How you explore your personal identity as an actor is consistent with the metaphor of air which is frequently described with a variety of words, such as wind, breeze, whiff or tempest.

I am both mature and young. I am mature compared to my great-grandson's artistic mentors like James Baldwin, Maya Angelou, Laurence Holder, Walter Dallas and Langston Hughes. I am young enough to appreciate that my work as an artist was ignored by the country that only began to accept that a person like me was capable of artistic works promulgated during the Harlem Renaissance and all that followed. As our friend, Langston wrote:

> "We younger Negro artists who create now intend to express our individual dark-skinned selves without fear or shame. If white people are pleased we are glad. If they are not, it doesn't matter. We know we are beautiful. And ugly too."

Langston Hughes's essay "The Negro Artist and the Racial Mountain" The Nation, June 16, 1926

In this centennial recognition of a watershed movement in the history of the arts in America known as The Harlem Renaissance I acknowledge that the molecules with which I fashion my sentences are inextricably linked to a particular moment, community and narrative.

It is impossible for me to separate myself or my work or the work of my family from this lineage nor do I desire to exclude Harlem from our conversation.

Your self awareness will direct your path as an artist. I write, as the artist of The Harlem Renaissance did, for the living and the unborn. I whisper silently to my great-grandson prayers for the trees who will be present to witness what we shall not and yet they will still supply the unborn with fresh air.

I write from and for the unseen. Our vibrations are interconnected and infinite. Our vibrations will remain and impact the quality of the air supply for the unborn. The unborn artist will breathe from the remnants of our air. Then these artists shall enrich the purity of the air that nurtures their dreams. Their dreams, visible only in an unconscious state, will sustain their world and the next. And so on.

Cora Summerhill
September 8, 2023
Galloway, NJ

AiR

Cora Summerhill
(1888 - 1960)

Chapter One: AiR

*It is like the AiR, Invulnerable.
- Hamlet by Wm Shakespeare*

Essalogue I.
Dream

DREAMS deferred are the most popular topics at cocktail parties and other social gatherings. "I always wanted to be..." is uttered often when people learn a bit about my great-grandson's background.

It is in response to those five words: "I always wanted to be..." that he began and continues to write and teach. He is grateful and fortunate that he has been gifted with experiences that others are also curious about exploring.

I, Cora, am clear that words may not teach and yet we are inevitably affected by vibrations. Teaching at best is the repetition of a series of sound vibrations hoping that the hearers will formulate an independent thought pattern of their own. Listen to yourself in silence and you will become your own teacher. That is the first practice that we will urge you to allow in your work and your life. Be quiet and still.

At some point I taught my great-grandson that he was an actor. Brother Safa, his English teacher at the Sister Clara Muhammad School in Philadelphia, was the first writing teacher who recognized that he had the potential to become a writer. My great-grandson continued to repeat that vibration to himself, until eventually it reached me. At this moment, I have six visible great grandchildren and a lot more great great grandchildren. None of the others have yet allowed themselves to publish any of their thoughts or internal sound vibrations.

My granddaughter, Jimmy, was a prolific writer of letters and a voracious reader, who frequently threatened to publish her sound vibrations into a book. It was only with the publication of my great-grandson's first book, Notes of a Neurotic (2004), more than two decades after high school that he allowed himself to become a story maker. It is with the publication of this book that we choose to share our shared approach to art after more than 33 years of listening and engaging with him about philosophy and art.

Your dream is your decision alone. My dream was my decision. What I allowed and what all my children, and their children allow is what we call "free will". You have heard yourself and others say that "I'm a fill in the blank with whatever you like, farmer, soldier, waiter, etc., but I want to be..." or "I'm a fill in the blank but I am trying to be..." an actor, for example.

Even when they are actually doing the activity that they want to do or are trying to do, sticking with the subject of this book, acting, therefore they are still merely a waiter trying to act or wanting to be an actor. When my great-grandson decided that he was an actor on-stage, off-stage, backstage, in the toilet, waiting tables, working at taco bell...everywhere...then that was the moment that he realized, in his words:

"I was living inside the unfolding of my dream."

When he made that one decision, his life changed and so did our relationship. When he decided who he was going to be then we, his ancestral energies, all lined up to assist him. This book is about his decision, what came before his decision, the consequences and most importantly, the implications for your decisions in your own life.

In this testament, organized into seven essa-logues, we share three fundamental points in any artist's life. The three divisions of the life of an artist include first who they were before they were an artist, then what they remember about the process of becoming an artist, and finally who they are now that they and the world both know that they are an artist.

In February of 2020, my great-grandson, Ray-Ray, yet known by a myriad of names, began keeping notes for this testament. I began composing the actual book in January of 2021. I intend to complete this revelation by the end of 2024. In 2022, Ray-Ray published a book of poetry that came to be called Autobiography of Ray-Ray & Other Ancient Ideas Like Hip-Hop.

All of the Summer Hill Seven writings are the most tangible residue of the air left for our heirs. Permit us to explore this conversation about acting as an art-form, rather than as a business, in a poetic conversation about three essential movements for the artist:

Movement 1.
What came before the decision to be an artist;
Movement 2.
The daily consequences of the decision to be an artist; and
Movement 3.
The implications for the decision in your life.

AiR

Movement 1.
Born to Act or Life Before Drama School

In a personal journal entry from November 28, 2020, Ray-Ray reflects thusly:

"Writing a memoir during a global pandemic feels familiar. I was born into the tumultuous world of 1960's poverty in the Black community of Albany, NY and my arrival on earth was on the 21st anniversary of D-Day.

The Vietnam war was in full bloom. Malcolm X and the President of the United States and his brother were all brutally and publicly slain. Riots were predictable in Black neighborhoods based on increases in temperature.

Chaos is the world I was conceived in, and it is the only world I have ever witnessed. Today, as I write, America teeters between fascism and a hope for democratic socialism while crouching in fear of an invisible deadly killer, known as Covid-19.

None of the effects of the tragedies that came before June 6, 1965 have left. These effects have grown more entrenched and are rapidly expanding. D-day was a great battle fought on June 6, 1944 in a war involving the world's greatest military forces. More than 150,000 Allied troops landed on the beaches of Normandy, France, as part of the largest seaborne invasion in history. The attack brought together the land, air, and sea forces of the allied armies in what became known as the largest invasion force in human history. The operation delivered five naval assault divisions to the beaches of Normandy.

Today the city of Tallahassee, Florida, where I began writing this book, possesses weapons far more deadly than the greatest of anything available in the 1940's. Do you know what else is greater or has expanded?

Joy. Peace. Love. Enlightenment. It is not ironic - it is inevitable. Only in a story is the contrast between obstacles and objectives truly appreciated. In theatre, we, the actors, become the physical embodiment of the contrast that results in a story.

A story is a result isn't it? A story is what is the remnant of an actual or imagined experience. The story of humanity - also known as the contrast of humanity is a result. This resulting story is multifaceted and may be told from an infinite variety of perspectives. As actors at the Professional Theatre Training Program (PTTP) of the University of Delaware we trained our instruments to play an infinite variety of characters.

Yes we want to portray our exact selves, the most difficult roles perhaps, yet we want to portray every self that is not our self too.

Some of us have a finite variety of selves we want to portray. Most of my colleagues at the PTTP are interested in a finite variety. The training must be for an infinite variety of roles because the story of human existence continues to expand. The actor must prepare for all that has ever existed before their birth and all that will ever exist. At the PTTP, Sandy Robbins, the director of the program, was very clear that we were endeavoring to 'access the eternal'.

Even though I noted the phrase 'access the eternal' in the brochure, it did not begin to mean anything until after I portrayed Gluttony, one of the seven deadly sins in the play entitled The Tragical History of Doctor Faustus by Christopher Marlowe at the Utah Shakespeare Festival in Cedar City, Utah during the summer of 2005.

My own approach to acting involves investigating the interior and exterior of a character. My actor movement training in the year prior to interpreting a sin in a state populated with adherents to a relatively new religious tradition, namely, Mormons, or The Church of Jesus Christ of Latter-Day Saints (LDS), was with Jewel Walker.

Jewel Walker is considered by some of the most celebrated American actors working on screen and stage today, including Albert Brooks, Cherry Jones and Ty Jones, to be one of the greatest acting teachers to have ever lived. In less than nine months Jewel Walker transformed my methods of preparing a character. I quickly discovered that creating the exterior of a character was the professional expectation.

In the same way that a prostitute is not expected to love her client, an actor is not expected to share the same emotional involvement as the audience. It is as unnecessary for an actor to feel what the audience feels as it is for an attorney to share the feelings or beliefs of his clients.

It is the external appearance that is for sale. However, it is the access to possibility that is one of the greatest benefits of live theater. In theatre, the players and the audience all bring all of their senses to the story. We use five or more senses to apprehend a single story in shared company and thus explode the multivalent possibilities of the story.

A well trained actor is 'cause in the matter' of variance at the service of the play. An actor's every movement must serve the play. Under the lights, the stage demands singularity of focus by the performers. It is in fact the singularity of focus of the actor that is the canvas upon which the characters or colors of the story appear. The interior life of the performer is best when it is either absent or quiet. Contrary to most everything I ever learned about acting prior to attending the PTTP, I am now far more effective when I quiet the internal monologue or chatter.

Dr. Naim Akbar, father of Black Psychology and internationally celebrated orator, described the experience of his speeches by saying "I had no memory of what I had spoken." He goes on to say, "it was as if another spirit spoke through" him. It is noteworthy that prior to attending college, Dr. Akbar was trained in theatre, in particular, he recalled his work with the works of Ibsen. Henrik Johan Ibsen, playwright and stage director who worked and created in Norway, remains an influential artist and is most known for his "realistic" approaches to theatre making.

A great deal of the actor training occurs from the distillation of stories told well, often and over long periods of time. Once you tell a story a certain number of times then it begins to speak for itself and tell tales of its own.

Such is the case with every story we tell ourselves about ourselves. Each new moment also offers access to the eternal. In this very moment as I conclude my writing session I learn that former heavyweight champion Mike Tyson is stepping back into the ring today at 54 to face Roy Jones, Jr. in another battle. Wonders never cease. Stories expand infinitely:

    My great-grandson wrote the above on November 28, 2020 and did not return to it again until January 7, 2021. I will leave the journal entries unedited to the extent that it does not cause you any confusion. These entries shall serve as exhibits in this case of "being air v. breathing air" herein submitted. These entries will also give you some inkling why it is essential that I complete this story with him. He cannot see himself and yet the artist who is responsible for creating himself first must find a way to step outside of the creation to complete it. I am the vehicle which allows Ray-Ray to see the creature he is creating.

    The journal entry is evidence of the practicing of the art of writing. The book, especially the poetry we share later is the evidence of the art of writing. The journal entries are evidence of breathing air. The poetry is evidence of being air. This book is subtitled - the poetry of art - because it is our sense that rhyme, rhythm and repetition is as fundamental to acting, dancing, painting, etc., as it is to poetry. In sharing our approach to art we urge you to think about your acting or art in the same way that a poet approaches a poem.

    Poetry is art. Hence, by the laws of mathematics art is poetry. Allow us to urge you to consider this perspective.

    Before we move on in the conversation, I want to pause here to tell you about my reaction to finding a baby in my mailbox. Actually, I did not discover Jimmy, myself. My husband James Turner Simpson found this innocent child with the most beautiful eyes that either of us had ever seen staring up at him when he went to collect the mail that morning.

That was on February 24, 1935 in the morning and all the baby was wearing was a cloth diaper. 'Lord Jesus, what in the world? What in the world are these young people doing? I know these are the end times now when folks is giving 'way children, putting them in mailboxes and carryin' on.' My husband says to me,' I hear tell in the big cities, people are finding babies in the garbage, sewer and everywhere else.' I could not believe it. He say, this little fella is lucky and might have a chance to survive, I hope he is asleep and not dead. Then my husband carried me to the midwife who was about 7 miles back toward the town because we lived out in the country.

As my husband hitched the buggy, I took this white baby quickly and said 'well, we gonna call the baby after you and take it straight to the local orphanage if it is still living. If it ain't living, I want you to be my witness that I ain't kilt no white baby and that you found it right there in the mailbox.'

I will tell you later about how I learned that the white baby was a colored baby who was my grandchild. I'll tell you about my daughter Millie, too, who was the mother of the white baby found in the mailbox. Millie was fast but she wasn't crazy or cruel so she did what she thought was right by the baby. You might think she was crazy or that something might have been wrong with the baby after that but lots of folks thinks that all of the

Summerhill family is a little bit crazy. I guess like most families, some is crazy and some ain't. Maybe when you learn more about our story you might understand why we react to certain things differently than other folks. It ain't just because of slavery either, like some folks like to claim. Cherokee people have some traditions that continue to be expressed by Summerhill folks and so do the Irish.

So, Ray-Ray, my great-grandbaby has wrestled with himself and the world over all these traditions and what you call instinctual responses to expectations from different corners of the world. He has written about the consequences to his choices before and in a personal Journal entry written on November 8, 2020, but typed on January 4, 2023 he reflected thusly:

"One of the many fascinating experiences that happened to me on the way to drama school was the time the NJ Medical School decided to indefinitely commit me to an insane asylum. My favorite stories are my own 'crazy house' stories.

This Newark story is pivotal because my narrative took a turn in Newark, NJ and in the squircular pattern of my life it led me to New Ark in Delaware.

Newark, NJ is to Newark, DE what…I don't know how you will end this sentence but in my memory it was…what hell is to paradise. We can come back to the excitement of hell later, this is a story about enjoying paradise.

The manicured lawns and perky coeds roaming around an intellectual environment is exactly to this minute my picture of paradise. Even now in my happily ever after I live and invest energy in an area with manicured lawns and perky coeds.

In Newark, NJ I was a legal aid attorney that wanted to be an actor. In Newark, DE, I was an actor that happily wanted to be an actor. And yet I was still an attorney and my educated judgment and factual observation skills are always operating in every interaction with other people.

As an attorney I have never been under the illusion that justice was anything more than an aspiration. I enjoy the verbal fight. Every opportunity to verbally joust is one I relish. Every verbal battle can be said to be in the name of justice.

At the PTTP I was caught between my instincts to simultaneously fight and flee and my desire to give and receive love. I love acting. I love the experience of stepping into the movements, syntax, occupation, etc., of an entity other than the one that I think of as myself. Yet the entity of myself is deeply affected by stepping into the entity of another. I am altered every time I step in and out of the entity of myself and others.

I love working on plays with gifted and talented creators six days a week. While in Newark, DE, I woke up and spent the entire period with the most talented and dedicated theatre makers I have ever had the pleasure of playing amongst. That is why Newark, DE was my idea of paradise because I had spent more than 10 years dreaming of the possibility of only being an actor. I was not a waiter and an actor. I was not an attorney and an actor. My complaints were the luxurious complaints of a full-time actor and were only understandable by other actors.

I will allow my fellow company members or classmates to remember it differently. Mostly I spent my days looking for an argument with other members of the company. By my second year almost everyone avoided conversation with me. I didn't notice. I was never a fan of idle conversation. Growing up as a self proclaimed teacher, every syllable was of consequence.

I was always thinking about my characters and my monologues. I always loved monologues. I still get lost in monologues. Richard Sheridan blew my mind with his play the Rivals. My initial reaction to the script was 'this will never work because there ain't no niggas in Bath.'

In fact that became my mantra during rehearsals. My mantra interfered with the rehearsal process severely. The rehearsals consisted of studying a live performance of a previous PTTP class performing Richard Sheridan's play. The Rivals was the second play that we worked on at the PTTP where we were being asked to learn the character from studying a video tape. I embraced the first time and resisted this second attempt with all my heart.

The first year of studying a video only worked for me because I was understudying Laurence Olivier. Whoever played Sir Anthony Absolute in this cast was brilliant yet this was neither Checkov nor Olivier. At that time, if you were a white person and I hadn't heard of you before then I automatically didn't like you nor care much about what you thought of me. The exceptions to this rule did not include studying a tape of a play that did not make room for my limited view of myself performed by white actors I did not know.

On general principle or "GP" as we say in my neighborhood of Arbor Hill, we don't vibe with white culture. We view white culture as the tool of the oppressor. I was into my 2nd year of daily immersion into the culture of the oppressor and I had enough. My body was rejecting these transplanted ideas about "accessing the eternal" and being "infinitely perfectible" and the fatigue was breaking down my resistance to the overwhelming feeling that I was being duped into swallowing European cultural traditions without critically interrogating the harmful long term impact on my psychological make-up, whatever that meant.

I decided that I would stage a one-man insurrection against the oppressor. I would do Sir Anthony Absolute in my own way. I refused to repeat the same blocking. I ignored the video tape all together. I wondered how deep the rabbit hole of white theatre went.

What had I gotten myself into? These people already knew these obscure plays. My classmates anxiously went to the casting board to see what role they were given. Some of my fellow actors were visibly more grateful and fortunate than others.

Casting, for actors, is one of those things where you are mostly happy to be cast at all. An actor, especially in a company, does not question their casting because you see it as a temporary assignment. An actor knows every life is precious. An actor treats every role as the precious gift that a life itself is.

Certain roles have an aura of je ne sais quoi - a certain sex appeal. I am not embarrassed to acknowledge that every role I was cast in during drama school

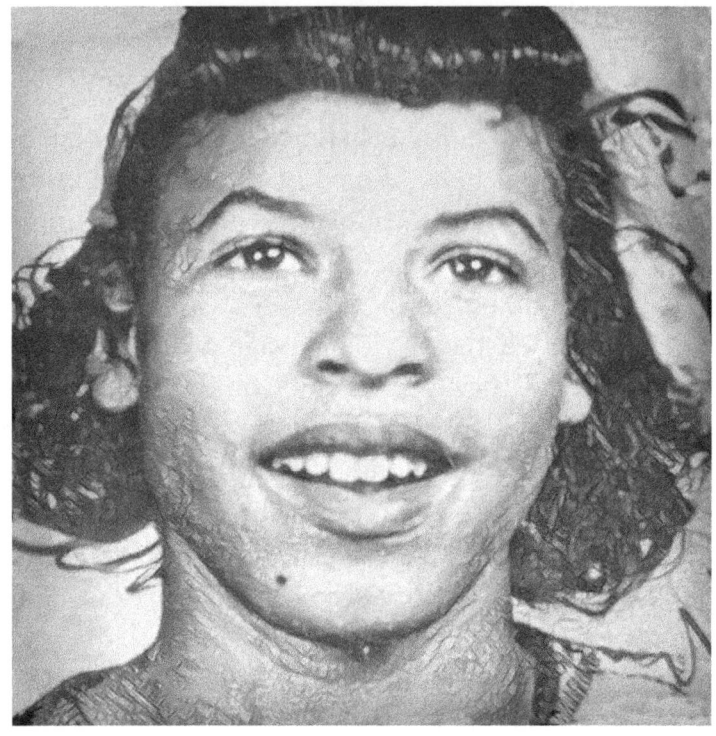

Jimmy Rebekkah Simpson (1935 - 2004).
She is the mother of the man on the cover and the grandmother of the baby on the cover. She is my granddaughter and the only daughter of my youngest daughter, Millie.

President Harvey Kesselman (April 22, 2023).
Dr. Kesselman (center) is pictured at his retirement party, and fundraiser gala for Stockton University flanked by two of his former students. Pictured on the left is Dr. Carlos Caballero, MD and my great-grandson is pictured on the right.

had a real regal sex appeal. I was the wise old lover. Chebutykin, Leonato, now, Sir Anthony Absolute.

Before Rivals, I was cast as Undershaft and after I was cast as Summerhays, two of Shaw's sexiest characters. Nothing is more magical than saying Summerhays played by Summer Hill Seven written by George Bernard Shaw. Sexy dudes. The ring of these names exude sex appeal both when read and when spoken.

On paper, Sheridan's Sir Anthony Absolute isn't particularly sexy but Leslie Reidel is a brilliant, no hyperbole, human being and master motivator. Leslie said some shit to me that was realer than real. He told me nobody else in the faculty wanted to work with me.

I understood their feelings. I was a lawyer. A lawyer only respects rules she agrees with. In theatre, status is everything. You can't have one guy who thinks and acts like he is better than everyone else. In my world, on the streets of New York or Newark, NJ, the only way you survive is to project absolute fearlessness coupled with callous indifference.

The more afraid I am, the more dangerous I am. The poemedy or poetic comedy of it as it occurs to me now is we are all afraid of each other and afraid to admit it to anyone. Inside myself, in my mind, I was always on the verge of snapping into a violent rage, choking someone or beating them with a chair. In fact, one of my favorite photographs from drama school is of me with my hands around the throat of my scene partner for our final showcase. I could kill Leslie, I thought more than once, but what would I have accomplished?

I just kept thinking and repeating in my mind that 'there ain't no nigga's in Bath why doesn't anybody else see this besides me?' Leslie made his final offer with less than 2 weeks until tech rehearsal at the last rehearsal before I was taking a rare trip to New York City.

I don't remember why I was going but I remember traveling with Luis Galindo while someone else drove. I told Luis that Leslie told me "to get my shit together or don't come back." Luis' face said it all: "it ain't fair but it is absolutely fair". "Don't come back." I was being threatened with being expelled from paradise. Theatre is probably the only thing where the possibility of fair and just is real. Luis did not need to say anything. He was a veteran of the 'NYC actor rat race' like me. He is brown, like me. We both knew there wasn't shit out here for men like us, even with an MFA from a great drama school.

We knew that we had hit the lottery by getting accepted to the PTTP. He knew this was the 2nd lottery win for me. For most people they saw theatre as the profession you pursued if you weren't smart enough to go to law school. Why was I taking a step down the status ladder? I was a varsity player coming to play JV. What happened? Was it too tough for me? I was suspicious and hopefully harmless. I was smart, talented and sexy. I was not to be trusted because I was a lawyer."

As you see from my great-grandson's own words, the fighting Irish blood is in conflict with the warrior Cherokee blood only to have to be refereed by the complacency of the patient African blood that can endure the unspeakable.

My great-grandson's first encounter with the air of theatre that sustains him was witnessing a performance of Oliver, the musical, at Stockton University. His experience on stage began with his very first play, which was an easter play, before the age of 7.

He doesn't remember anything about his very first experience on stage except that he attended rehearsals before his mother fled from his step-Father, hitting the road, so to speak, long before the actual performance took place. Jimmy used Ray-Ray as the decoy for her mission to return to Ohio to take custody of her other children who were left behind in Cincinnati.

Seven years after the easter play, Ray-Ray gave a David Walker speech on Black History month in 9th grade. He was in Schenectady NY in a large auditorium standing before what felt like to him thousands of people as he allowed David Walker's words to take over his body.

He breathed air and David Walker spoke of the birthright of the Colored Citizens of the world with each exhalation. Immediately thereafter, Ray-Ray became a youth Imam (Muslim minister) that went into adult prisons and preached the Quran to these men. He was a boy who knew everything and nothing at the same time.

AiR

Raymond Bernard Larkins (Ray-Ray) (circa 1976).
This photo was taken in a municipal park between Albany and Schenectady, NY by Ray-Ray's mother Jimmy Rebekkah Simpson.

Ray-Ray, changed his name legally at the age of 17 to Raymond Abdul-Alim Akbar and was an early volunteer for the Committee to Remove All Images of the Divine (CRAID) and it was CRAID that allowed him to experience life as a "street preacher" which is a particular experience that only a few men will ever enjoy. Street preaching is how Jesus spread his message. Jesus was a "street preacher" before there were paved streets.

Ray-Ray decided to call himself Alim in college and graduated from college at Stockton which is where he was introduced to Western ideas of art. Art as a profession and way of life is decidedly bourgeois because poor people do not have the luxury of choosing work, they must accept whatever work they are offered to receive their daily bread.

After graduating college with a liberal arts degree, he attended a professional school at Princeton University to study public policy. The school was known for many years as the Woodrow Wilson School. After the televised and very public murder of a man with hair like lamb's wool and skin like bronze named George Floyd, Princeton University changed the name of the school to the School of Public and International Affairs. Ray-Ray or Alim remains curious about the conversations that led to this decision. The motivation of the school is obvious because the story of progress is marked by powerful men, mostly, making concessions by abandoning seemingly deeply held beliefs and principles to appease a new generation. Power peacefully concedes to demands when it finally comes to recognize and accept that they are out of sync with the narrative of those over whom they claim power.

After leaving or dropping out of Princeton, my great grandbaby went to law school at New York University School of Law. He went to law school because the white baby found in the mailbox, who was Ray-Ray's mother, Jimmy, wanted him to become a lawyer. Ray-Ray has always been indifferent to the law. He did not know any lawyers as a child. He never even spoke directly to the lawyers who represented him in his juvenile delinquency cases. The idea of the law as an instrument of human progress was not something that spoke to Ray-Ray but like a good Summerhill, he obeyed his mother and found something to look forward to in an experience that was in his mind, no better or worse than any other minor demands that parents make of children.

Ray-Ray had a friend in college, named Carroll Robinson who became the first graduate from their alma mater to become the President of the National Black Law Students Association (NBLSA). Ray-Ray decided that he would be the next person from Stockton University to become the President of NBLSA. Ray-Ray had without any acting training learned the most important lesson an actor must learn and that is "motivation". Motivation is fundamental to every conversation yet, once you master acting it becomes the least significant question in the process.

Long before you master the process of acting, there is only one of two possible motivations that a professional actor cares about: 1) the money and 2) the feeling of living inside the part or the character. You either want to do the part and/or you want the money from doing the part. The actor must find their own motivation. It is a myth that characters on paper have specific motivations different from the motivation of the actor. The mumbo jumbo about motivation relates to what is popularly and scholastically known as 'script analysis'. Acting is a profession older than the idea of "actor motivation".

If your acting teacher wants to quibble about this then send them to my great-grandbaby and he will set them straight very quickly.

Ray-Ray learned about the craft of acting from being cast in a bus and truck tour of a Pulitzer prize winning play by Charles Fuller, A Soldier's Play, during the second semester of the second year of law school. He was paid $450 per week plus room and a per diem to portray Corporal Ellis on the tour from as far north as Maine and as far south as South Carolina. He had not mastered the craft yet he had become aware that there was craft that existed independently of inspiration.

He worked with and carefully studied the practices of several masters of the craft on this tour. Apprenticeship is the only road to beginning to understand the craft of acting. Acting is an impossible combination of voodoo, witchcraft, magic, alchemy and countless other mysterious artforms. However, inspiration is the foundation upon which the craft of acting exists.

Going to school for acting without first practicing is completely an ass backward approach. If Ray-Ray had not practiced the craft before studying or attending drama school, he never would have been admitted to the PTTP nor would you be reading this book. This book, ultimately, is about inspiration and how to experience it, manage it, and allow it to use you as an actor."

Canopy Roads Theater
in association with Poemedy.com
presents
A Raisin
in the Sun
by Lorraine Hansberry
March 22 - 24, 2013
with
Summer Hill Seven
as
Walter Lee Younger
Friday & Saturday Shows at 8:00 PM
Sunday Matinee at 2:00 PM
For Tickets contact:
Monticello Opera House
185 W. Washington, Monticello, FL 32345
850 -997-4242
www.monticelloperahouse.org
Member Discounts Available

You will not read a book about acting, attend an audition, learn a line of dialogue without inspiration. Yet with inspiration alone you will remain in doubt about your choices as an actor. My great-grandson learned this lesson from a production of a play written by Leroi Jones who later became Imamu Amiri Baraka.

At Stockton, when it was still mostly known as a state college in southern New Jersey, Baraka was invited to speak. Like many young men, Ray-Ray was indifferent to Baraka because he never met him nor knew anything about him. Ray-Ray knew about Carter G. Woodson and the significance of Black History month from the performance where he spoke David Walker's words in Schenectady, NY., and so he dutifully attended this event. When he arrived it was standing room only and the atmosphere was filled with a rare sense of expectation. Black college students, faculty and members of the community were crammed into a large lecture room in the C-wing of Stockton college.

A black man who appeared to be ancient, probably in his late forties, wearing a painted grimace approaches the podium after a lengthy reading of accolades that meant nothing to Ray-Ray who was mostly raised on American TV, Christianity and Black Muslim iconography.

The man begins to read from a pamphlet. He states the title, a reference that even at this moment Ray-Ray doesn't understand, then begins to read, and Ray-Ray thinks, is that what everyone came to hear, this old guy reading. He looks around the room and all eyes are glued to the old guy reading, listening with a particular ear. The audience listened, apparently with their hearts because many people closed their eyes.

Then Baraka said the line that eventually captured Ray-Ray's heart, changed the way he breathed the air in the room and it was only two words: 'Hey Coach!' Each time Baraka said 'Hey Coach', the air crackled and Ray-Ray's heart beat faster. Ray-Ray had heard those words, Ray-Ray had said those words. Ray-Ray knew the reference to the television show about the white savior coach, entitled The White Shadow.

Ray-Ray was not aware and may only now understand that his relationship to the society he has been raised in has been shaped by his willingness to call upon a "white shadow" for the best strategy. Harvey Kesselman was Ray-Ray's white shadow. At the time, Ray-Ray did not understand the idea and significance of the white shadow. He did understand by the time Baraka had finished that Ray-Ray was no longer Ray-Ray. Ray-Ray had become Alim.

In the 11th grade, while a student at Trenton High School, Ray hired a paralegal to complete the legal name change paperwork. The cost was approximately $250.00 and his father, Joseph Larkins never responded to the paperwork that the law required to be sent, but his mother, my granddaughter, the white baby in the mailbox went to court with him. Joseph and Ray, despite living, for the first time in both of their lives, in the same city, had barely spoken to each other. The lack of response to legal paperwork from a son that you have not attempted to communicate with, requesting the court to change his name from the last name of his Christian Deacon father to an Arabic 'Muslim' name on its face seems consistent.

Yet, perhaps there is more to the story that Ray-

Ray does not yet know, in the same way that he does not yet know the significance of the Baraka poem that led eventually to the decision for him to want to perform in the Dutchmen or become a poet who reads words to audiences. Alim is a name that connotes someone who is engaged in learning. It does not however mean someone who is all knowing. The name is for someone that wants to learn more. Alim, Ray, both of these people live in one body.

So by the time Alim becomes an attorney admitted to practice law in the state of California and decides that now that he has kept the promise that his mother made to the shopkeeper in the Arbor Hill candy store, it is time to keep some promises to himself. He begins with Baraka. Alim decides that he wants to play Clay in the play, Dutchmen written by Leroi Jones, who changed his name to Amiri Baraka.

The play, Dutchman, practically speaking seemed ripe for an actor who is operating with very little craft, and a great deal of inspiration, having just completed a twenty-two-year mission given to him by his mother. The play only requires two actors and the plot is based on two people who randomly meet on a NYC Subway train. In the same way that the white female antagonist kills the black male protagonist, Alim's enthusiasm for the theater was murdered by his failed attempt at producing and performing in this Los Angeles production of this play in 1995.

Dutchmen deprived Alim of air because he did not have the craft to know how to continue breathing when the demands of the text assaulted his mind. He allowed his heart to stop beating when his mind stepped in to defend him from further trauma. Here is the point, air moves in, that is inspiration, yet unless you exhale, you and your acting are in danger of a certain death.

Indianapolis was the city where Alim fled to once we resuscitated his dream because we knew the purpose for which he came to this life to fulfill.

AIR is all I am. Air and quantum bits of carbon, hydrogen, oxygen, nitrogen, and phosphorus.

It is March 29, 1970, following an Easter Sunday matinee production of the film Superfly in Albany, NY. My grandbaby, Jimmy, is wearing a plum-colored dress with white shoes and a matching hat with a blue rose pinned on the left side.

Ray-Ray is dressed in a charcoal gray pin-striped zoot suit with black marshmallow-colored heels and a burgundy hat to match his handkerchief. It is Easter Sunday in the ghetto of Arbor Hill, N.Y., and in his five year old mind he lives at the center of the universe.

His mother, feeling especially excited about this day, asks him if he wants some candy from the corner store on Lark and 2nd Streets. The boy makes his selection, when Jimmy goes to pay, not surprisingly, the owner is very complimentary of their smart outfits.

Ray-Ray was surprised by the owner's question because no one had ever asked him about his future plans before and yet with his quick Irish tongue, he answered without hesitation.

"What do you want to be when you grow up, little boy?"

"I'm gonna be a pimp!"

And before Ray-Ray fully enjoys the final p in the word, Jimmy yanks his arm so hard that he is airborne and nearly out the door. As Ray-Ray glances at his mother's face, now bright orange, he witnesses her scream at the giggling woman who owned the store, "he's gonna be a lawyer!" Jimmy was gone, the owner loudly laughing and the door purposely and perfectly slammed shut.

Jimmy still loves telling that story repeatedly even until this very day. She told the story long after November 1992, when Ray-Ray was admitted to the California Bar.

Jimmy enjoyed telling it even more after Ray-Ray had fulfilled her prophecy. Ray-Ray went to the movies, alone, to mark the occasion of passing the California bar and watched X the film, produced and directed by Spike Lee based on the Autobiography of Malcolm X by Alex Haley and the script One Day When I Was Lost by James Baldwin.

Alim felt relieved, calm, and peaceful more than anything as he sat alone in a nearly empty theater.

Alim had decided that whether he passed or failed this three consecutive eight-hour day-long bar exam he was not going to take another standardized exam again for the remainder of his life. We shall see about that.

In his own words, Alim explains:

"From the age of five until twenty-seven I had been jumping through a series of flaming academic hoops with the one known goal of satisfying my mother. This burden followed me from juvenile detention centers to group homes to jail cells to insane asylums to churches to mosques to discotheques and after 22 years I still was not sure what was in it for me.

Lawrence Graham, the writer, had described a law degree as a fuck you degree by which I understood him to mean that anyone who questioned your intellectual capacity would have to concede that you were capable.

In the film X, the boarding school headmaster, a white man asks young Malcolm the same question that the owner of the candy store asked me 22 years earlier.

"What do you want to be when you grow up, Malcolm?"

"I want to be a lawyer..."

"But you're a nigger Malcolm, niggers can't be lawyers."

Suddenly tears formed in my eyes hearing those words and witnessing this scene. No one had ever suggested that being a lawyer was anything less than absolutely possible for me.

Most of the people diligently and actively supporting my mother's ambition for my life were white. Many of them, like my mother, insisted, in fact, that I must be a lawyer. Until that moment I had two heroes and they were in order, Jesus Christ and Malcolm X.

I asked myself did I still want to be a pimp? The answer was yes.

Along the 22-year journey from that moment I decided I wanted to be lots of different things including basketball player, politician, writer, college graduate, religious teacher, actor, writer, husband, father and so many more.

At that moment I knew I had to become an actor because that was the best way to fulfill all the desires for my life.

In 2007 when my only son was born and I received a Masters in Fine Arts in Acting from the University of Delaware's Professional Theatre Training Program I was finally satisfied that I had achieved both my dream and my mother's dream.

I have spent and continue to spend the remainder of my life supporting other people in understanding, embracing and pursuing their dreams.

I have come to understand that having a dream is my primary goal and pursuing the dream is my secondary goal.

Stockton University is the college where I first planted the seeds of my original dream. The so-called 'accomplishments' are the harvest of the seeds planted here more than 35 years ago. I return to sow seeds for my son and the next 35 years of my life. If you or anyone else discovers benefits from me pursuing my dream do not blame me."

SUGGESTED ACTIVITY 1:
Set your timer for 15 minutes and look into your own eyes in a mirror without speaking or moving for the entire period. Look and listen for the quality of air that you attract and allow to flow through your body.

Production photo from A Raisin in the Sun in Tallahassee Florida (circa 2013).

Essalogue II.
Investment

The difference between spending your life and investing your life is the difference between an insignificant life and a fulfilled life. You know people who make statements like 'another day another dollar' or 'same shit different day' or 'another day above ground is a good day' and they are wonderful people who have not created a purpose for themselves. They may choose at any moment to do so because the past does not equal the future, although it is a pretty accurate predictor in most cases of the future.

History, the academic discipline, promises that if you pay attention to the past then you will be able to chart your present movements in alignment with your purpose. But that is mumbo jumbo. The fact is, as philosophers agree, 'purpose' is not essential to life. Purpose adds joy to life. Joy is indescribable, especially to the perpetually melancholy. Joy is flavor. Joy is a rainbow with no regard for the pot of gold. Joy is the smile for no reason.

Until you have a dream, your very own dream, not one given to you, the chance of experiencing joy is unlikely. Forget goals, visions, objectives, etc., that is mumbo jumbo compared to a bonafide dream. Dreams are the lungs of your spirit-being. As you spend time alone, in silence, looking at yourself breathing you are fulfilling the dream of your spirit before you had a body. All your spirit dreamt of was having a body. I know. I am a spirit working through the body of my great-grandson and I dream of once again having a body.

But this story is not mine. I do not have a body. I have a great-grandson with a body and a most powerful spirit, and a set of dreams that inspire me to give him attention. Your dreams give you purpose. Once you have a dream, that is enough. The dream alone will give you purpose. The purpose will give you joy. My granddaughter, Alim's mother, as a girl was always talking about her dream of having 10 babies. We laughed at her so much as her tiny little fingers picked cotton in Florence, Alabama and she would go on and on about how her "ten little babies were going to be helping her pick her cotton and they would pick so much cotton in one day they would never have to pick cotton again."

She became the mother of 10 children because of her dream. We did not attempt to dissuade her from her childhood dream. We were mothers, fathers, grandparents, picking cotton with her and preparing her for the life that we expected we all would have. We were cotton farmers. We found joy in our work. Our dream was to have a family and our land to farm. My dream was to sow and make garments with my cotton.

My art was making clothes. I am what you call now a costume designer. I am an artist. I designed the costumes of my seven babies, Tenny, Hugh, Emmett, JT, Lottie, Burlee and my baby, and the mother of the white baby found in the mailbox, Millie.

I am also what you call now a chef. I created recipes that fed my family and many families and that is how I began to engage with my great-grandson, pictured on the cover of this book, in 2017 because when he bought a house in Tallahassee the garden was dedicated to his mother but he called the kitchen, 'Cora's Kitchen' to commemorate me.

I taught him how to cook with a skillet. I tried to teach him and he listened as best as he could considering I ain't got a body. We are still working on it. My great great-grandson, the baby on the cover of the book, is my taster. If he can eat the meal that Alim prepares then I gives it the thumbs up. I have given many meals the thumbs down, too many to count.

Purpose. Dreams. Joy. These are for an actor the mechanics of inspiration. You must cultivate your joy. You must choose a dream you can see inside your mind. You must take on intentionally, on purpose, to bring into being what you see inside your mind. Investing in your dreams, with your time, and other available resources is the only way to bring the dream into being.

After the failure of the Dutchmen, Alim abandoned acting as his purpose and instead decided to invest in a new purpose. The new purpose he decided was that he was going to own a business. Although his ideas about exactly what type of business were not clear he began investing in becoming a businessman.

He did not know that it was too late to abandon his dream of being an actor because he had already fully manifested the specifics of that dream. The dream of owning a business had to follow the dream of being an actor, in the same way that being an actor had to follow the dream of being a lawyer. This book is about being an actor thus the next movement in this story is about the biggest investment you can make as an actor, your choice of training. Acting is nothing if it is not learning.

Death of a Salesman at the REP of Delaware (circa 2010) with Steven Pelinski (left) as Willy Loman and Alim (right) as Charley.

Hence, it is only natural that a man who legally changed his name to the Arabic word for "a man of learning" would choose a purpose that requires daily intensive learning.

Seven as Lincoln in Topdog|Underdog by Suzan-Lori Parks directed by Walter Dallas (circa 2007)

Movement 2.
Becoming an Actor or Drama School

In a personal journal entry from April 18, 2021, my great-grandson reflects thusly:

"I spoke with Matt Burke this week for the first time in a couple of years. 'Unstoppable' was the word that he used in our 're-enrollment conversation'. He believes we were in the 'Iron' something pub when the conversation occurred. Enrollment conversation is a phrase we learned from our study with Landmark Education in Philadelphia.

I said, according to Matt Burke, 'I'm out!' That was my 'ghetto' way of saying that I am quitting the PTTP. Matt Burke encouraged me to reconsider without judging me. My perspective was, 'who cares' if I leave. Matt cared. Matt said, you are already a hell of an actor and he didn't doubt that I would continue to succeed. He understood my fragile ego and my unspoken sensitivity.

Matt was an actor and we were improvising a non-fiction scene that would have real-life consequences on the most important aspects of my life. He would listen until I stopped speaking. Then he would pause and listen for his thoughts to arrive. After receiving it in its entirety he states: "Man if you stay and get what is to be gotten here, on top of what you already have, then you will be unstoppable."

Unstoppable! How exciting is it to know that someone believes in your talent to the extent they would support you and simultaneously encourage you to push past the comfortable to find ease? Life gets very easy once you become unstoppable.

In the Quran, among the descriptions of the righteous is that they shall not grieve. When I remember that moment it lives as an angular point in an infinite sequence along the *Sirat al-Mustaqim* (or straight path) to the fulfillment of my purpose - your purpose - our purpose.

Matt Burke was showing me that once you conquer these demons from which you are fleeing "You shall have no fear, nor shall you grieve. For you, Akbar, there shall be gardens with rivers flowing beneath them." Yes, the divine was using Matt as the instrument and voice of destiny.

We both knew but neither needed to state that we carry our demons with us. I came to the PTTP to again confront the demon of Shakespeare's language. I came to prove finally that I was greater than Shakespeare or any that dared flex with the 26 symbols we call the English alphabet.

"These things and greater shall you do."

Wordsmith? Wordmaster? Wordgod? Unstoppable. The future existing in our conversation contained the story of the boy who was regularly told to "shut up" but some day would be begged to utter a single syllable. In that conversation, that little boy was front and center.

His eyes lit up. He said "Yeah and nobody will be able to tell me what to do ever again." There will be many other angular moments between the first play and the final play when Xalimon, my son arrives. Each point carefully constructs a complete squircular path that leads here.

A path that leads to you holding these sets of

words. The moving finger writes and having writ, moves on is how I remember the translation of Khalil Gibran. The breathing actor lives and having lived moves on, is how I experience my own life.

I am a mere moving finger of an almighty deity. I submit my whole self with no expectation of comprehension. Leslie Reidel was among the first people to hip me to the notion that comprehension of rhetoric is the "booby prize".

Understanding written or spoken words is for an actor merely a starting point. In the web of what we grossly refer to as words are infinite worlds. The opportunity for word painters exists in our exploration of pigmented varieties and shade distinctions. For example, the color red for a painter is a universe. Likewise, the sound of the word red is for an actor also an infinitely evolving universe. These distinctions are more than mere metaphors. These distinctions are far more tangible than the entirety of the common law.

Where the law was artificial, arbitrary, and symbolic, the professional theater is regimented, reliable, and distinct. Every production scientifically approaches an eternal theme. Each team of theater scientists brings distinct backgrounds to a set of symbols.

In the legal system, the outcome of the process is opinion. In the system of theater, the outcome is eternal, ethereal, and yet tangible. In the law, witnesses are asked to recount an occurrence. In the theater, we collectively witness and experience action under the eye of heaven.

The event lives eternally in the hearts of the witnesses and with all whom they share these experiences. In that way, theater is truly unstoppable."

Frankenstein, a stage adaptation of the novel by Mary Shelley (circa 2012) Scott Mock centered as Dr. Frankenstein and Alim under the cover as The Creature.

At Stockton University, which was still a state college then, Alim took his first formal acting class with Pat Hecht in the fall of 1984. At the State University of New York in Binghamton, in the fall of 1991, was where he took his next formal class in acting, seven years later.

After law school, he auditioned for three graduate programs in acting because everyone told him that "you have raw talent, but no technique". True, Alim not only did not have it, Alim did not know what it was that he did not have. He was under the mistaken impression that it was something that he could learn the way he had learned the law, public policy, political science or African American studies.

Alim auditioned for the State University of New York at Binghamton's two-year-old MFA program, for NYU and the Yale graduate school Masters of Fine Arts in Acting. It would not be the final time he would audition for acting graduate degrees. It would be the first (but not last) time in his life that he would walk into a room and after 5 minutes or less of speaking, leave with more than a hundred thousand dollars in the form of a fellowship to study acting.

Alim chose a scene from Julius Caesar and from The Sign in Sydney Brustein's Window. Gene Lesser asked him to make an adjustment in the latter monologue. He did, then Lesser told Alim about his background and asked Alim about his. Then the white shadow begins to take charge of the conversation:

"I saw Sydney Brustein on Broadway. They used

a white actor for that part. Where else did you audition," the shadow wants to know.

"NYU and Yale" Alim said flatly.

"If we offer you a full ride with a living stipend for all three years, would you take it now?"

Alim laughed aloud at the idea that he would not take a bird in the hand over 'two in the bush' because Jimmy did not raise a fool. "Yes."

Gene Lesser made the magic move, he held out his hand and Alim took it. Just like that Alim was given a full three-year fellowship to study classically in the manner that an actor must eventually or forever live with the lack of such training. That an actor can become rich, famous, and successful without such training is beside the point. The actor with some kind of repertory and/or classical experience has a richer experience of the craft. Comparisons always collapse.

Alim immediately told his law school roommate, and a few close friends about the fellowship but who else could he tell that would not call him a fool for walking away from a very lucrative Wall Street law firm offer to work with wealthy Wall Street banks to "learn how to act?" The truth is he was embarrassed by his own choice of a dream. Certain types of success continue to embarrass Alim.

Alim, like most men, is selfish in his ambitions and private, almost mysterious about his motivation. Ray-Ray learned to be mysterious from Bernie, his Daddy, who was known as a gambler - a street hustler who imparted perils and pearls of wisdom to the boy learned from Pearl St. and other Albany gambling spots, like "when you have a hot hand, don't walk away from the table." Ray-Ray reflexively thinks, what is the next game he can win, even before he finishes winning the game he is in that moment playing.

Acting, the craft requires killing the previous moment with the next moment, which Alim will learn from his friend, and acting coach Jewel Walker. In this moment, when Lesser asks Alim whether he wants the fellowship, Alim kills that moment with the next syllable he utters. Yes. That sound is perhaps the most powerful sound a human can make. Yes. Say yes. Say yes to your dream. Say yes to every investment in your dream. Say yes to every obstacle confronting your dream.

Something actors have in common with other actors is they gamble and they say yes. Denzel Washington took a big gamble when he accepted the role of Brutus in Julius Caesar on Broadway in 2005. He did not do it for money, necessarily, although his net worth and market value both increased subsequently.

An artist must only think of out doing or surpassing themselves. After law school, Alim thought, what will outdo being a lawyer? Plenty of Presidents of the United States were lawyers, in fact perhaps too many. Ronald Reagan was the first President who had ever been an actor. None had ever been both. This is still true.

Alim remembers the smell of the air in the 21 by 17 square foot room in New York where he went to audition for SUNY Binghamton. It was a stuffy and dusty room. As a country, even in New York City, most buildings still permitted cigarette smoke inside in the early 1990s. Someone had recently smoked in this room and the carcinogens were still fresh in the air, as Alim entered. When he left that dusty room he was floating on the urine-scented air of Times Square. He glided above ground from Times Square to Washington Square Park imagining what studying theater was going to be like. Alim's mind stepped in to protect his heart from the anticipated criticism and rebuke from his classmates and other shadow people in his mother's dream.

"Can I defer, one more year from Princeton" Alim asked himself and then the University administration who responded with certainty.

"No".

"Can I defer my offer at the law firm for a year" Alim asked himself and then the partners of Orrick, Herrington & Sutcliffe law firm, who responded with delight.

"Yes".

"Can I defer the completion of my final paper for my independent study from law school?" Alim asked Professor Randy Hertz, his law school white shadow, and the shadow shouted with glee.

"Yes".

Alim was not really that disappointed about not completing a Masters of Public Affairs from Princeton. He enjoyed the people, and the classes and found his crowd among a few of his fellow Princetonians (a proper graduate would not use that term) yet, the work did not excite him as much as the unknown possibilities associated with being a bona fide actor.

After all, he was already a professional actor. He had received money for performing for two and a half whole months. What was the big deal about training? Nothing. Unless you choose to make it a big deal. Alim

AiR

chose to make it a big deal and thus every day of his life, especially after he eventually received an M.F.A., 16 years later, has been a big deal. He started writing this book to you and for you to explain to you why it is a big deal.

Alim, with my help, wrote this book for you so perhaps you may find the type of richness and wealth of spirit you will have access to once you embrace the poetry of your art. You have an art. You are art and you have art. Have you embraced the poetry of your art? Even when your art is poetry, the poetry of your art is a distinct element to be identified and embraced.

Your art is yours to select. The poetry is a refined understanding and restatement of your given narrative. Who gives the narrative? Your narrative is created by you, and your co-authors, including parents, teachers, family, shadows, etc., and is only readable upon reflection.

Now, breathe in the air. Exhale. Repeat. There is tremendous story material in each breath of air. The poetry is mostly a result of crafting air. When spoken, the poetry results from allowing the air to vibrate the vocal cords.

Much of what Alim has learned and wants to share is about the air that vibrates the vocal cords.

"Do not speak the Ha, allow the Ha to speak you." This was the instruction given by the vocal instructor at the State University of New York. Alim's law school trained brain did not have any concept of a 'ha' nor if his brain were to learn what a 'ha' was his brain would never let said 'ha' to do him. The entire endeavor was beyond bizarre.

That was the beginning of Alim studying the mysterious science of acting. It is a practice he continues even as you read these words. Alim wants you to recognize that the air is the tangible matrix through which all of the material world is connected. It is this tangible and material connection that allows for the possibility of art. The awareness of the connection permits a personal poetic expression of your distinctiveness.

SUGGESTED ACTIVITY 2:

Set your timer for 15 minutes and get a pillow, place it under your head while you lie flat on the floor simply breathing in through your nostrils and exhaling through your mouth while thinking the sound 'ha' but not saying the word.

Essalogue III
Association

  You will morph into an amalgam of the human energy with which you most engage. My grand baby, Jimmy, Alim's mother did not teach nor ever learn the significance of carefully and consciously choosing "the company that she kept" because people liked her immediately. Often she fell into groups because of the men she chose. She did choose men that talked of good and sounded like the down-home blues of W.C. Handy, the father of the blues.

  Such a man was Alim's father, Joseph. Although Ray-Ray (Alim) spent very little time with Joseph as a child, in fact only about 5 days, however as an adult, Alim made it his business to learn about Joseph. Alim intentionally chose to associate with Joseph because Alim understood that the son was a reflection of the father, regardless of whether the son is aware of it or not. The son is created by the father ejaculating air and fluid into the mother.

  Hence, the fluid and the air on the particular moment of ejaculation is associated with creation resulting from the ejaculation. Mortals account for these particulars with cataloging zodiac signs. The ejaculation that created Ray-Ray occured in September of 1964 resulting in his birth occurring in June of 1965. Essentially, the period that Jimmy carried Alim was equivalent to the typical academic year calendar, September through June.

Alim was conceived over a single academic year. Alim was born to teach. He is most creative during that period from September through June of each rotation around the sun. Alim declared himself a 5%er or "poor righteous teacher" and began associating with other GODS, as they are known. He has consciously associated himself with GODS from age 13 until this very moment.

Association occurs on many levels. Certainly when you are in the presence of someone then most likely you are associating with them to some degree. It is important to your art that you carefully and consciously choose every material association in your life. Your art will be significantly impacted by the air and the quantum matter that you come into contact with, especially when you are creating a work of art.

The theory of quantum entanglement deals with issues invisible to the naked eye yet measurable nevertheless. Air includes subatomic particles that of course contain protons and electrons. When scientists measure these subatomic particles they have observed that even when separated by immeasurable distances the connections made between protons, neutrons, and electrons remain unbroken.

All these elemental subatomic particles impact our discussion about art and acting. As we share a different moment in the background of my great-grandson's life we are identifying the subatomic principles that you as an artist want to consider in relationship to your work. You must learn about your instrument, which for the actor is the arm, leg, leg, arm, head, and trunk encasing the vital organs from which these extremities issue forth.

You must understand the subatomic structure and origin of your instrument before you can ever hope to master yourself, which is the doorway to mastering any creative endeavor. You must learn about yourself before you were assembled and all the particulars that led to your being assembled. Even long after a person ceases to exist in physical form you will have access to their energy and subatomic material, as my presence in this conversation attests.

Especially as an actor, you must know your own self, before you have any hope of creating other "selves". In the language of acting we call the other "selves" characters. We interrogate the player (or actor) about the character they are interpreting. We ask the player who is the character, what the character wants, where is the character, when is the character living and why are the actions and words of the character meaningful.

These are the questions that my great-grandson has learned to ask because he continues to investigate his answers to these questions. This is what distinguishes this conversation about art from any other that can ever occur. This conversation is a singular conversation between Ray-Ray, the seed of a man, and Summer Hill Seven, the fruit of a man.

Summer Hill Seven is the invention of Raymond Abdul-Alim Akbar. Raymond Abdul-Alim Akbar is the conscious outcome of the interrogation of the quantum entanglement with GODS. At birth, and we shall now call our great-grandson the name that we and the other members of our family call him, Seven, was closely associated with people concerned with god, righteousness, divinity, and religion on a subatomic level.

In his early understandings of the conversation about being GOD rather than merely worshiping or having a God, we confront the pre-existential question of how God or Consciousness comes into existence. To be GOD, God must be self-created. Our conversation does not relate to being God yet it very much relates to the metaphor of God because every actor is asked to create a being.

The ability of an actor to create a being is the measure of their worth. The more persuasively you can create a fully realized being the more you are believed as an actor. The more you are believed then the more opportunities you have to create. Your responsibility as an actor has been greatly overestimated. In this conversation Seven speaks of acting in the most lofty terms because that is his proclivity. You may feel differently about your art. God has blessed the artist that practices their art form, created by them and for them. Poemedy is Seven's art.

Actor
(Job Description)

Time is not the sun going up and down. It is not a clock. It is not a calendar. Time is an eroding, infinite mystery. Time is in fact, a son of a bitch.
  - Preston Jones, Playwright

The playwright makes the story and the world. The actor makes the moment. The audience makes the meaning.
  - Summer Hill Seven, Actor

Learn the lines and don't trip over the furniture.
  - Spencer Tracey, Actor

Know your words and pray to God.
  - Claude Rains, Actor

Trust your intuition and just go in and do it.
  - Bette Davis, Actor

(Sources of the first and second quotes come from actor, director, and artistic director of Vs. Theatre in Los Angeles, Johnny Clark. The remaining three quotes come from a book by the Oscar-nominated actor Burt Reynolds entitled But Enough About Me: A Memoir.)

The single greatest benefit of attending drama school also known as professional theater training is the opportunity to associate with the GODS of theater. Ray-Ray had only tasted this in the less than nine month period when he was enrolled in Binghamton's Master of Fine Arts program at the State University of New York (SUNYB).

The taste and the enigma of breathing while thinking the "ha" but not saying the "ha" and letting the "ha" do you rather than doing the "ha" had become entangled with how he thought about speaking. My great-grandson has been making speeches since before he was delivered by my grandbaby.

He was told to shut up so much that by the time he began his work at the University of Delaware's Professional Theatre Training Program (PTTP) it became necessary for him to see a specialist. At SUNYB, the faculty said there was this "thing" in the sound of his voice that impairs his speaking voice. Finally, at the PTTP this "thing" had been properly diagnosed by Deena Burke and the program paid for him to be treated by the top specialist in the field in Philadelphia, Pennsylvania.

How Seven had adapted to speaking allowed him to be heard and yet shielded from any perceived threats. He spoke in the back of his throat which was wreaking havoc on his vocal cords. If you combine this subconscious habit with his proclivity for smoking cannabis and eating late, the doctors predicted that he would destroy his vocal cords very quickly given the production schedule of the PTTP.

The specialist ran a telescope through his mouth down into his stomach and created a video that showed the erosion of the walls of the throat cavity. The molecular structure of Seven's voice-making tools was on the verge of ruination.

Immediate action was needed and Seven was never more cooperative with a team of professionals. He remains to this very moment, two decades later, as committed to preserving and strengthening his voice making tools.

The air that you share will shape you from the inside outward. The proof was undeniable. The evidence of drama school's impact was as Sanford Robbins had promised, viz., the creation of players that would become "unrecognisable to themselves". In this one subatomic area was one of the greatest transformations for Seven. Seven no longer recognized the sound of his voice.

Given that he was isolated from all prior associations by a significant distance, the new entanglements with the GODS of theater began to take hold on his behavior and experience of sound. He had already understood how to let the "ha" do him while working with Nina Murano in his private studies of the Meisner Approach to acting. However, now, in the PTTP, in the promised land of drama school, he became the "ha".

In a personal journal entry from November 11, 2020, my great-grandson reflects on his association with drama school thusly:

"My son was born during the rehearsals for Topdog|Underdog. Walter Dallas directed me in this well received performance. The year my son turned 13, Walter Dallas transitioned to ascend the highest heavens, no doubt.

Yet the connection between all of us continues to grow. Xalimon my son ran track in middle school. On November 10, 2020, he won first place in a race. I saw the footage on video. The race was very close. In the final seconds, Xalimon sprinted ahead.

In my experience of those moments, you must decide what is more important.

Is what is holding you back more important or can you let go of everything and allow yourself to manifest. By the time Xalimon was born, I understood that idea even better since I was in my final year at the PTTP.

Working with Walter Dallas was my final production of drama school. The race that my son won will forever remind him and even confirm to him his capabilities. It is not something someone else can give you.

I came to drama school out of a desire to compete. I want to win. I want to win it all, all the time. Perhaps that is how I experience my life. I play each moment and I seek to perform at my peak in every moment.

Once a person gets that experience they will return to the source of the peak feeling again. Drugs, alcohol, and sex are all examples of places or sources of peak feelings. Fitness, art, surfing, and perhaps we can imagine that all of life is 'seeking a peak feeling'. I imagine the world I live in as a place where life is always perfected.

A place where the good guys have enough bad guys to chase, and the anti-racists have enough racist to keep them motivated. Ying and yang. Boogie and bang bang. In drama school, every moment was exactly like the final moments of Xalimon's race last night.

In fact, in the final semester when Xalimon was born I was cast in at least three plays. I would arrive home from rehearsal at about 11:30 pm and be immediately energized by the sight of Xalimon.

Usually, Xali was asleep when I came in from rehearsals. His mother was either asleep or enjoying much-earned quiet time since I was essentially gone from 9 am. Xalimon was born in mid-March and our performance of TopDog was in early April.

I wasn't off-book yet so when I got home I made myself something to eat and while I ate I worked on my characters. I was in my final semester of drama school. My process for working on characters was very elaborate.

Only a dancer would be able to tolerate, endure, dare I say, suffer the utter inconvenience of me.

I know a little about the way some actors work. I have made videos about some aspects of my process. It is the love of the process, the love of the race, the love of the game, and the love of the chase that matters to my son too.

It is also what has always mattered to me since I can remember. It is the thing I am chasing even now as I share these two squircular stories about being handed the baton of black theater by Walter Dallas and my son's love of the chase.

He dramatically won the race. With me as a father and an accomplished artist for a mother, he possesses an unspoken if not innate sense of drama and panache. He demonstrates his ability to strategize and make decisions. He inspires me.

13 years ago it was only "The Chase" that inspired me and at the top of my peak performances list

was the character of Lincoln in TopDog|Underdog. The spring before the coldest winter when I stumbled into the audition for the PTTP, I began plotting to produce a production of this same play TopDog|Underdog written by Suzan-Lori Parks.

Sean Slater, my friend and an American filmmaker met with me in a diner on the east side of Manhattan. We read the whole play—Sean read Booth, I was Lincoln. I didn't even have a place to live but I had other resources. I was hopeful and prepared to play Lincoln.

Nevertheless, I was shocked when Nadine, the PTTP coordinator involved with selecting the PTTP season sent me an email asking me a question about TopDog while requiring that I not disclose the communication nor was I to conclude that I would necessarily be cast.

Later in my career when white-owned theater companies would do the same kind of thing regularly, I understood that this pattern has deep roots in maintaining order. I appreciated Nadine's confidence in me.

I can easily keep secrets because I don't tell other people's business nor do I mind other people's business. I also choose what I want to make my business. You might mistakenly believe something is not my business.

TopDog|UnderDog was my business. I made TopDog|UnderDog my business the moment I read about it in the Village Voice. I was living with Shellie in Queens Village. Shellie witnessed and was entangled with the tumultuous quantum transition from Legal Aid attorney to full-time artist.

I went from a regular lower middle-class income to no income during our relationship. The monetary change was the least of it. The priapism was undoubtedly the most painful part. I never knew of priapism until I experienced the painful erection that lasted for several hours until the physicians gathered around gawking at the Black penis pointing northward asking me if I wanted them to drill two holes into it. Shellie witnessed me consent despite the warning that this very well may be my final erection. The story of my penis merits a story of its own. This is a story about acting. Shellie is fundamental to both stories.

The relationship we shared with Shellie itself is ripe for further artistic exploration. Shellie is a model. She is a gifted beautician. She makes people beautiful including herself. She made me discover beauty in me where I only saw ugliness. She nurtured my relationship with my hair and skin. She reminds me of my mother. Her spirit is calm yet highly sensitive. Her anger is lethal. Shellie was a very generous fan of my acting work.

When I read Jeffrey Wright in The Village Voice saying that he was an actor for very personal reasons it moved me. I didn't have a reason that I could articulate because it was unreasonable for me in my mid-30s to leave a law job and start auditioning. I picked up something from what he said and what he did not say.

When I sat in New York's Public Theater in the obstructed seating by a thick cement pole I knew. I knew that his reason was very similar to my reason. This personal reason for doing this work is the unwillingness to accept anything less than peak performance in every moment of life in association with people who are taught to deny your humanity. We call that the "Black actor's dilemma".

Working with Walter Dallas on TopDog was the way the Universe also known by many as Source confirmed my arrival into the happily ever after. In the moments of the chase when John Gruber, stage manager for the show, interrupted the TopDog rehearsal to announce that I must now go be with the birth of my child began the squircular collision of subatomic quantum particles entangling into multiple miraculous manifestations all around me.

In the moment of the chase, when Xalimon easily emerged from Afua in the moment of his birth and on his own power raced from her tummy to her breast —there was a kaleidoscope of images exploding in my heart—including faces of my mother—my grandmother —my classmates—my teachers—my preachers—my enemies faces of people not even identifiable—all of humanity meeting at the gate between all of life and merely material life.

Just like last night when Xalimon too, chose to win that race—he was the sperm who chose to win the race to his mother's egg and when he entered our life on March 12, 2007, began our happily ever after.

Today I can feel that Walter Dallas is as proud as he was on the day he first met Xalimon."

Essalogue within an Essalogue: Name Unborn

All works of art are created without a name and the name arrives out of the necessity to recall the work of art.

The first monumental and unexpected moment occured on the due date which was March 7, 2007. No baby. No water breaking. Water breaking, even now, occurs to me as the most polite way of saying that you are urinating on yourself. There may be more to it, but for now, I know enough about birth, so until I am confronted with the opportunity to witness it again, I don't ask those questions.

I have never met anyone nor do I expect to meet anyone with my son's name. My son's Mother, or Ummi, was so persuaded by everyone and the superstition of how you are "carrying a baby," during the pregnancy that nearly all of our conversations about names were focused on female names. We began our conversation by agreeing that we wanted a historical female name. During the pregnancy, we agreed and cooperated on "breathing preparation for the child-birth experience" and the idea of natural childbirth.

"Inhale...exhale...inhale...exhale....what about Harriet..." I ask. Ummi, on the exhale exclaims ..." too old-fashion..."

I'm running through an unmemorized list, "Shirley Chisholm Akbar..."

Ummi takes a deep breath, and exhales, "Maybe..." and then "what about Coretta Scott."

I scrunch up my face, "I love what she stood for but it is not what we stand for necessarily. Inhale...Clara Muhammad Akbar might be closer to our values, what do you think?"

Ummi continues to breathe and shakes her head no. Then on the next exhale strikes a vein of gold "...Sojourner"...and we say "Truth" together.

We quickly, thereafter, agreed on the name, Sojourner Truth Akbar. We both loved the name for different reasons.

Ummi says "she is excited by the strength of the name" and the "significance of the historical figure, and her message".

I tell her "The poetry of the three names is also compelling" and we are both pleased yet curious why we have "never met nor heard of anyone named after such an important historical figure". We are proud to be the first to "re-birth such powerful energy into the world".

We began to refer to our yet unborn child as Sojourner. We prepare for the scheduled date of the birth of Sojourner. We completely agreed that we still did not want to know the gender of the child. Ummi is a dancer, who prefers to improvise her choreography around a theme. I am a student of acting on stage, who lives for the moment, especially when something unexpected happens. In this case, I am equally as excited when the expected does not happen.

Sojourner is expected on March 7, but she does not arrive. March 8, she did not arrive. March 10 and 11, and Sojourner is still at large. I am excited. Ummi is not. What I remember most about the days after March 7, is that Ummi's Mother had relocated from Florida to Delaware and has been living with us since March 1, 2007. I was in class during the day until 6 pm and in rehearsal in the evening from 7 pm until 11 pm. On March 8th, Ummi, me, and Ummi's Mother realized that if we happened to have a boy, then we would have to begin negotiating over boys' names. Everything with Ummi is a negotiation in which I am expected to lose.

I was expecting a negotiation, I was shocked when there was none. Ummi is only concerned with getting this girl out into the world to breathe on her own.

"Feel free to speculate, and theorize on your own..." Ummi sighed heavily, "just be ready when the time comes".

I did not question it because I knew that Ummi would have the final say so I merely enjoyed the temporary illusion of freedom and set about making a list of all the possible male names that I would select.

After a list of 100 or more names, I developed a criteria for eliminating names from the list. I immediately eliminated any names that were obviously related to any of my names. I have no less than ten different names myself so that criteria reduced the list significantly to a core list of about 15 names.

On the morning of March 11, 2007, before class I checked in with Ummi, "Here are the possible choices for boys' names" if, in the "unlikely event, the child is a boy" adding "What do you think". Ummi is growing indifferent about names focusing rather on when will this baby finally arrive? I am focusing on learning lines, and blocking for the Pulitzer prize-winning play Top-Dog|UnderDog directed by Walter Dallas and written by Suzan-Lori Parks.

The play takes place in a studio apartment in which two brothers, Lincoln, an actual Abraham Lincoln impersonator, and his younger brother Booth, the actual tenant on the lease of the apartment, "temporarily" reside together after Lincoln is evicted from his home by his wife. Lincoln is a former street hustler, in particular, he was known as the most prominent NYC three-card Monte player until the fatal murder of his best friend during a hustle gone wrong leads him to reform his ways and choose an odd yet legal source of income.

Thus on the remaining list of alternative names for Sojourner Truth Akbar are the names of the character I am portraying in the play, Lincoln and James Baldwin. James Baldwin is on the increasingly short list of names because Suzan-Lori Parks was a student of Baldwin and he encouraged her to write plays. Walter Dallas was best friends with James Baldwin and was working on directing a new play James Baldwin was writing at the time of his passing. I had met and shared a private dinner with James Baldwin and four to six other people when I was a freshman at Stockton University.

In the fall of 1983, I am unexpectedly invited by my rhetoric and composition professor who declined the offer to dinner at the Ram's Head Inn with two upperclassmen, Charles Price, financial aid officer and head of the Black Council of Faculty & Staff at Stockton University, James Baldwin and Mr. Baldwin's travel companion. I am a first-semester freshman and don't know any of the guests nor had they invited me. I knew of Mr. Baldwin because I wrote my senior thesis in High School about him.

He was flattered but more notably he was curious about how I came to be interested in him. When

I told him that I graduated from Sister Clara Muhammad School in Philadelphia, his curiosity grew further. As fast as I was able to answer his questions, he fired another one.

In between bites, Baldwin says "Tell me more about what is going on with the Nation now that Wallace has taken over".

We are in a private dining area of an exclusive five-star restaurant with white linen napkins, the shiniest silverware I had ever seen in my life, a full place setting, white waiters and I lacked the vocabulary to describe such a scene because I had never witnessed it before, even in the movies. It would be many years before I would ever experience opulence and service on this scale again. I sat directly next to James Baldwin, on his right and he was on my left. His companion was on his left and the other three guests, two men, and one female student also vied for the attention of the great man. I did not know that I was expected to behave in any particular way other than the polite well-mannered way that my Mother and the adults in my life had insisted that I behave. I wore my only suit, gray with white pinstripes, wrinkled white shirt, and a solid blue knit tie. My suit was a gift for graduation from high school from the group of parents from my Mosque who had sponsored my tuition, fees, and transportation to Sister Clara Muhammad School.

I spoke as a representative and a proper young Muslim man was expected. "It's called the World Community of Al-Islam in the West not the Nation of Islam anymore and we practice the religion of Al-Islam in the traditional way that Muslims all over the globe do by adhering to the five pillars of belief in one God, prayer, fasting in Ramadan, charity, and the pilgrimage to Mecca. I am writing a paper about it this year in my rhetoric and composition class."

Mr. Baldwin asked me if I would send him the paper when I finished it. I agreed to do so and continued to eat my chicken breast before it disappeared as the soup and salad which I had barely touched during the inquisition. I was able to gobble down a few quick bites while the other guests asked questions and made clever comments that I did not understand. I listened and learned that a writer was expected to have a quick and clever response to every question. Mr. Baldwin was in that moment exactly as he is whenever I watch him now on screen, in a dark business suit, white starched shirt, thin black tie, poised, curious, authentic, supercilious, and incendiary. When I think back to the moment, I remember that Mr. Baldwin wore the chip on his shoulder with panache, boldly and proudly. He might agree with me that the world had placed the chip on his shoulder and he made it his own. I knew about the relationship between him and his father, a subject that he explores in his writings but I had no such relationship with a father to compare it to, thus, I could not appreciate it as a source of fuel for my pursuits. After leaving the fine dining establishment, we returned to campus where under stage lighting, Mr. Baldwin shared extraordinary stories about his relationship with Malcolm X and Dr. King et al., during the height of the civil rights movement, as I began to glimpse some sense of possibility for a Black manchild, like me and my unborn son.

James Baldwin Akbar was a real contender for my unborn child's name; far more meaningful than Lincoln Booth Akbar. Finally, Ummi's dad weighs in with Khalil Gibran Akbar. Now, my tiny bit of autonomy was beginning to slip away. I had to find a way to insert myself back into the unnecessary selection of the name of the boy who would never be born.

I forwarded negotiations by adding another name, so now the fictional baby had four names. Her name was Sojourner Truth Summerhill Akbar. Summerhill was the name of the patriarch on my mother's side of the family. Ummi agrees it is important to include this name, especially since my parents were both deceased before the conception of our child. It is a small but significant concession won several days past the due date. The Khalil Gibran idea, however, was gaining traction with Ummi and her mother. I began to revisit the list of boys' names that were now scrawled on a piece of paper in my hand on the white metallic refrigerator in our one-bedroom plus den apartment. The den was the presumed bedroom of the unborn child. No signs of pink or blue were evident. We still agreed we did not want to know the gender.

Finally, to regain some sense of hegemony over the process I proposed a new rule that the name of the boy could not be a replica of anyone living or dead. Ummi concedes to the amendment of the rules of the baby naming game. That eliminated James Baldwin and Khalil Gibran. It did not eliminate Lincoln and Booth because while they were representative of historical figures, in the case of our son, they would more represent what was going on in the life of his parents, especially his father, at the time of his birth.

Secretly, I wanted the name to contain within

it one of my names and I unilaterally decided on the fourth day after the due date that it must begin with an X. X in mathematical language is used to represent the unknown. The X also represents the unknowable identity of millions of Africans stolen from that continent and brought to this continent of North America, some being dropped along the way in the Caribbean Islands where Ummi was born, to labor for generations in the worst conceivable circumstances. The X, when questioned about it further by both Ummi and her mother, I explained, "captured and included the spirit of Sojourner Truth and her declaration of 'Ain't I a Woman' broadening it perhaps to a more inclusive question, viz., Ain't I a Human? This fact," I declare, "will be the enduring question in our child's life".

The beginning of our child's life was riddled with the unknown. We did not know the gender. We did not know when he or she would breach the portal of mortality. Moreover the entire Professional Theatre Training Program of the University of Delaware was all on notice because of our collective commitment that this child would not be born without the presence of the father. This was among the most beautiful experiences of a kind of communal restorative justice I have ever witnessed. Hence, every role that I was cast in had an alternative plan for performance except for Top|Dog. I had understudies on the ready waiting for the call to go to the hospital. This was the final and most active production schedule for the entire 3 years of the MFA program. That this was a priority says everything about these particular theatremakers.

On the refrigerator, in the meantime, is a list of

names beginning with the letter X followed by "alim" - which is half of my legal middle name and various forms of a third syllable, in some cases. Xalim was a very likely choice, yet it was still too similar to my name for both me and Ummi. In that moment the family name of someone on the Summerhill Family tree pops into my mind as a perfect justification for this increasingly bizarre experience of naming an unlikely and unborn child. Solomon. The strength of the name and the story of the biblical figure on its own was enough to persuade both of us that it was the best choice.

Solomon Summerhill Akbar.

I expect that Ummi will soon push back on that name and she does. Declaring that "I am not represented in this name". I came home between classes on March 10, 2007, and our unlikely son is now known as Solomon Truett Summerhill Akbar. "Truett", Ummi explains, "is the name of one of Alvin Ailey's original dancers". I say it once, twice, then in Jamaican patois and then I simply and without ceremony state "I love it". Ummi giggles, licks her full lips, rubs her full belly and says it again with an even broader smile "Truett". We both like it because it captures the ring of truth that we bonded over in "Sojourner Truth". In the Jamaican patois of Ummi's Mother, Truett and Truth share a very similar sound. On March 11, 2007 our son was named Truett Solomon Summerhill Akbar.

We are so close to a final agreement, but I felt like now I had negotiated myself from my son's name and carefully examined the list to see if with an alternative spelling I might reinsert some more of me back into my son's story. Ummi is not excited about a son with a name that begins with an X both because of the politics associated with Malcolm X, part of my revealed secret, and because she thinks it sounds and reads more like a superhero rather than an actual person.

March 12, 2007 the child was born male, healthy, naturally, and received by Ummi, his Grandmother Cherry, the midwife, and me with love and wonderment. Ummi got used to the X.

Our superhero is now 17, and his passport reads Xalimon Truett Summerhill Akbar, his mother calls him "Tru-Tru", I call him "X" but he prefers to go by Xali.

Summer Hill Seven

AiR

Opening night of Topdog|Underdog with Seven holding Xalimon, John Gruber, stage manager, and Cameron Knight as Booth in the Roselle Center for the Arts (circa 2007).

After Xalimon was born, Seven performed Lincoln in TopDog with his new son in the audience. My daughter Millie, and granddaughter Jimmy and I, Cora, all enjoyed Seven's performance as we watched along with Ummi and Xalimon. Within two weeks he graduated from the University of Delaware's PTTP with the bold declaration from the Board of Trustees of the University of Delaware that Seven had mastered the fine art of acting.

Poetically speaking it was the way the Universe or Source said to Seven that you have mastered your instrument and now you are free to demonstrate it with how you co-create. Now, go forth and co-create, with the baby who is newly and freshly entering into your material world. Go and be a father. Become one of us. You have made men, in your work. You have made yourself. Make with us a greater creation than yourself. Make your son.

In the second year of drama school, before portraying, Lincoln in TopDog, Seven was cast along with Mic Matarrese to interpret Undershaft from the play Major Barbara, which was written by George Bernard Shaw. Two actor's cast in two parts that they would switch between in alternate performances. That is to say, in one performance Seven was Undershaft and then the next, Mic was Undershaft.

This was the role in which Seven was asked to perform more words than any other character he had ever created with less than half the rehearsal time. Unlike many of the requests that Seven reluctantly accepted at the PTTP, he eagerly relished the opportunity to utter, with his still healing and developing new vocal sounds, every syllable of Shaw.

Even now, Seven is planning an occasion to utter again these sounds that give access to an eternal and important existential conversation. He asked Sanford Robbins (Sandy) in November 22, 2021 what he remembered about the production from 2006 and Sandy wrote him back the following:

Dear Seven:

Happy Thanksgiving to you and yours!

I have nothing to share from that experience but I do remember what a fine job you did in the production. There are few roles that are as challenging or as rewarding as Undershaft, that is for sure.

I wish you and your family the happiest of holiday seasons.

Love,

Sandy

Summer Hill Seven

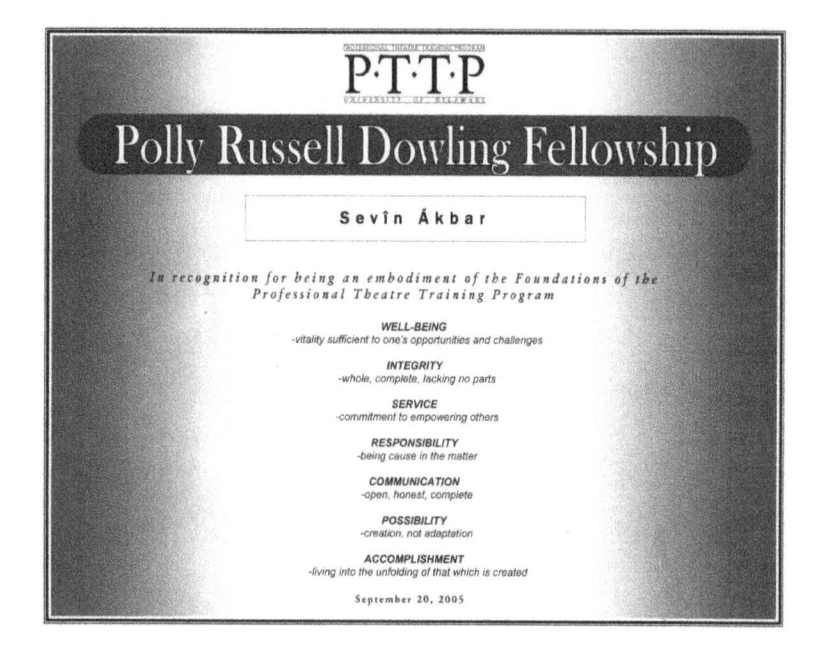

P·T·T·P
Polly Russell Dowling Fellowship

Sevîn Ákbar

In recognition for being an embodiment of the Foundations of the Professional Theatre Training Program

WELL-BEING
-vitality sufficient to one's opportunities and challenges

INTEGRITY
-whole, complete, lacking no parts

SERVICE
-commitment to empowering others

RESPONSIBILITY
-being cause in the matter

COMMUNICATION
-open, honest, complete

POSSIBILITY
-creation, not adaptation

ACCOMPLISHMENT
-living into the unfolding of that which is created

September 20, 2005

Seven's approach to fatherhood is entirely based on the training that he received from the PTTP. I, Cora, am a teacher of acting too. My quantum DNA material is intimately entangled with Xalimon and thus we are one. As such, I am teaching myself how to live under the present circumstances with the participation of Seven.

Art. Air. Poetry. These are the subjects of this conversation that must be revealed in language that severely limits creativity unless we unlock our connection with universal consciousness.

The exercise that we suggest to engage with all of what best captures the remnant of Seven's lessons from three years of drama school training is popularly known as breathifyer or "breath of fire".

SUGGESTED ACTIVITY 3:

Set your timer for 15 minutes and begin to bounce by bending and straightening your knees rapidly. At first simply inhale and exhale as you bounce. Then beginning with your highest pitch release sound with every bend of the knees. After you start with the high pitch then move to a distant pitch that resembles the sound of calling someone at a distance from you. Then move to directing the sound toward your nasal passage and release the sound through your nasal cavity. Then move to directing the sound, that is to say, the air toward your mouth. Then move to directing the air toward your chest. Then move to directing the air toward your abdomen. As you move from directing the air in different directions listen for the quality of sound that the air creates as it changes direction and focus depending on where you release it from within your physical instrument. Your emotions and ideas will be altered based on quantum adjustments that you attract and allow to flow through your body. Summer Hill Seven has created a video on YouTube that demonstrates this exercise because this is where he begins working with every new pupil of acting with whom he exchanges air and ideas.

Chapter Two: The Poetry

The playwright makes the story and the world. The actor makes the moment. The audience makes the meaning.
- Summer Hill Seven, Actor

Essalogue IV
Technique

Approaching Acting in 2025
Breathe.
Body: brain - heart - genitals.
Imagination.
Speaking: Just keep talking.
Thinking.
Style: Time; pace.
Chakras et. al, make the invisible tangible.

Poetry is to literature what the "moment" is to an actor. The actor is called upon to craft a moment in the way a poet is expected to craft a poem. The actor is not expected to feel, or tell the audience what they feel or think. The audience needs to feel and make meaning from the moments of their lives. The playwright is expected to give the actor dialogue, perhaps a plot, but certainly the parameters of a particular world.

The actor's body of work is the tangible evidence of their technique. Body. Body of work as a phrase feels pretentious to Seven. How does it make you feel? Does it feel poetic?

The tragedy, comedy, and freedom of awareness that your technique is something that you see in hindsight inspires Seven to continue to refine his technique.

Your body of work is the tangible evidence of your technique. Hence, your technique will never be completely known by you. Instead, if you document it, your technique may be available for others to share.

The work teaches us, as performers of the work not as the teachers of the work. The teacher listens truthfully and behaves truthfully. You choose to allow experiences and say yes to opportunities for experience. Learning is inevitable, yet the rate of learning varies wildly from actor to actor.

Some actors learn too well and too quickly; while others may safely be considered a "slow learner". Such a learner is Seven. From this point, we will leave you with Seven to reveal the rest of the book.

Class of 2007 of the University of Delaware, Professional Theatre Training Program, with Adrian Hall and Matt Earnest in the Pool Room where we began every morning with Yoga, breathing, voice, and speech preparation for the day.

"I wish the stage were as narrow as the wire of a tightrope dancer, so that no incompetent would dare step upon it." Johann Wolfgang von Goethe (1749 – 1832): Wilhelm Meisters Lebrjahre; book 4, chapter 2 (this quotation was framed and hung on the wall in Sanford Meisner's office).

Movement 3.
Being an Actor or Life After Drama School

SOLDIER'S PLAY was the play that led me to drama school so it was only perfect that immediately after graduating I was cast in the role of Sgt. Waters performing on the same stage as one of the greatest known actors, Eleonora Duse, the Italian actress who is quoted as saying "The actor wears an invisible garment which he takes off only at death."

The acronym M.F.A. to Luis Galindo, my classmate and I meant a "mother fucking actor". Each year we earned a letter. After the first year, I was a mother; and after the second year I was a mother fucker; finally, upon graduation, I was by every measure a mother fucking actor.

After passing the California bar, a three, eight-hour day exam, I took private pride in my achievement. After graduating from the PTTP, once again I took a moment of private pride that my dream was achieved. Both achievements were the beginning of a new journey. Each beginning was a breeze—air circulating onward.

The notion of developing my own method of acting was something that I went to drama school with and my three years were spent on developing a precise method. This book was written to document certain aspects of that method and share it with anyone interested in learning from my experience.

Drifting

A lawyer loses his mind and finds love.
Letting go of letting go
And holding on to now Forever.

Summer Hill Seven

Kennedy Center Performance Poemedy*

Now. Romeo, don't know what he don't know
Now! Very Now and live
Is the winter of your discontent
Made glorious. Summer, a son of New York
And the clouds that lowered on this house
Named for the slain POTUS take notice
And dig, dig, the irony of the two households
Both alike in Dignity in fair DC once known
Chocolate City, Dig, dig the Ukrainian Romeo
Romancing the Russian Juli and the
Palestinian rams tupping the Israeli Ewes
Where the slain friend of the slain POTUS
Gave notice about the blue Black boy
Holding hands with source of his own demise
Alike bewitchèd by the charm of looks,
Tempering extremities with extreme sweet
Two households both alike? Tupping opposites.
Dig, assimilation, right Saint Lorraine
The new Negroes ain't comfortable with
The new new Negroes and declare them rude.
Rude am I, in my speech, nappy are my locks
Little blessed with the soft phrase of peace
Supercilious to embrace this chip of wood
You have placed upon my red shoulders
(Indigenous chant of woo woo woo)
Mumble, mumble, mumble in the dark
Babylon, crumble, crumble, crumbling…
Look out Mr. President don't be stumbling
YOLO, we so close, though now is the time to

AiR

Make the "Captain Kirk move".
Boldly go where no leader has ever gone.
Mumble, mumble, mumbling.
With the full Monty on.
Temp'ring extremities with extreme sweet.
Let hands do what lips do and
Say it loud.
We stand for ...peace.

*This Poemedy was performed by Seven in the Kennedy Center for Performing Arts as part of Bard & The Beat. (circa 2023)

Good Morning Neighbor

I don't be drunk
Like how you be drunk.
You don't get crunk
Like how I get crunk.
They don't know funk
Like how we put down the funk.
He is in a place that is sunk
Like the way treasures are sunk
Deep in the belly of an ocean
Trapped inside a locked trunk
Waiting to be rescued by
New-age pirates or a young drunk punk.

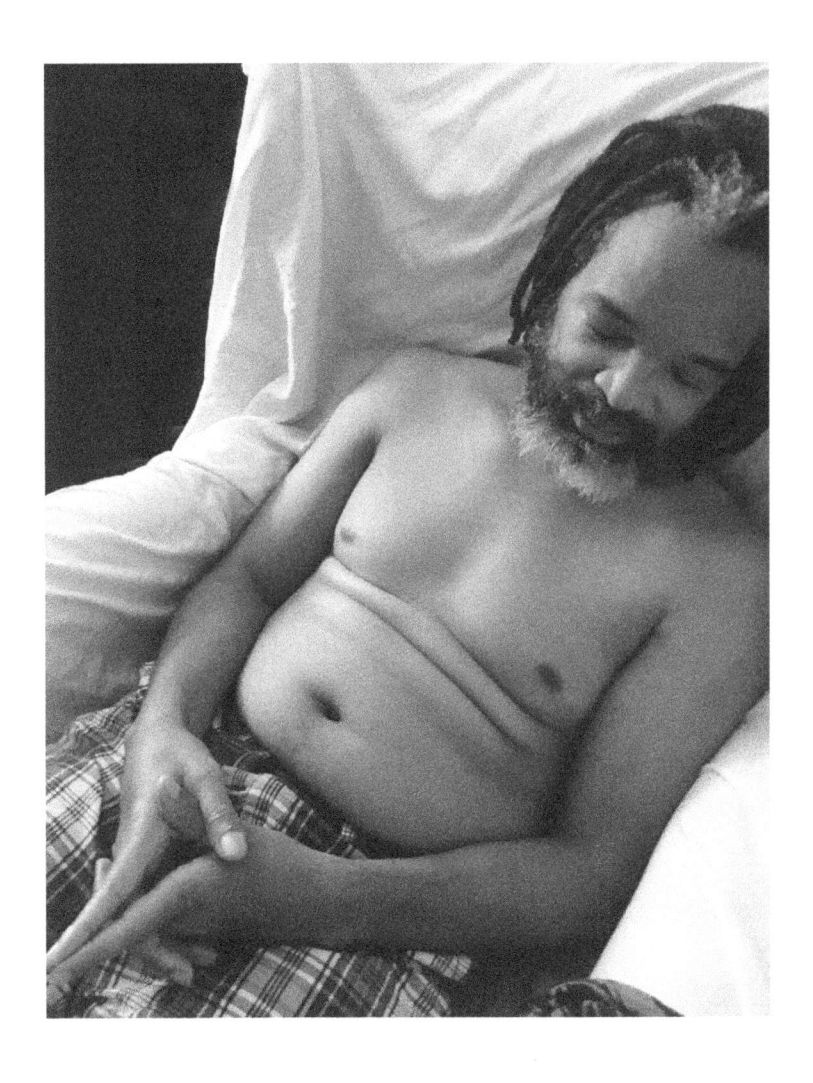

AiR

Summer Hill Seven

Hiding

It's crowded at the top
The true solitude is right
Here at the very bottom.

Haters

You know those people
That only give you doubt
Without benefits
Ignoring all your prior
Accomplishments.
Love them.

May 20, 2022 in Tallahassee

Let us segregate in public
To celebrate integration
Let us congregate slavishly
To celebrate emancipation
Let us gather publicly
To despise one another
Privately, discreetly, uniformly.

AiR

Summer Hill Seven

AiR

Here

The only way
I can
Go anywhere else
Is to be somewhere.

Just me, Nekoma

Is it just me or
Did someone ask you
If you know anybody who
Wanted to buy a chainsaw
On your walk around your
Neighborhood too?

Crystal's Haiku

I'll be your arbor.
Commune with all my branches.
Fresh air. Summer breeze.

Summer Hill Seven

Best time to make love

Now is best
And the next best time
Is the now that
Immediately follows now.

Homecoming

Ohm is the sound first heard
The first home for the first sound
Came about after the sound
Was sent out, lost and left out.
I am now that sound first
Sent out, lost and left out
Circulating the circumstances
Instead of penetrating present
Proclamations.
That sound summarizes all
Of me. The sound most evident
In that which evades me even
When ostensibly engulfs me
Hah! Ohm! Mother. Womb.
A location I pretend with
Mortgages, leases, certificates
Of birth. Yet unable to come.
To arrive. To reside. To remain.
Meet me there I promise you
I'll never be there.
I will forever be coming despite
Zip code on my debit card
Despite the gps setting.
Despite Siri's declaration of
You Have Arrived.
I won't. On earth arrive ohm.
Ohm has gone. I circulate
Until I am ohm.

Private Signs

Signals from
The 6th day of the
6th month of the
7th decade of
1900s at 6am
Received on
The 9th day of the
8th month of the
8th decade of
1900s at 10:37am

Reunion

My ear is nuzzling your
Heart-side breast as
Your spine caresses earth.
Heavenward you face stars
Inward we dance to steady
Tom-Tom bass percussion.
Few words for our soul's discussion.

Everafter

Time and once again the
Poets lead us to utopia
Only to be disturbed by
Mortal avarice's frenzy.
If I must choose between
Possessions and belonging
After longings leave - all of me
Belongs among all you possess.
Confessions, testaments, sacrifice, giggles, wiggling
Work, play, dance, shout
About freely & happily.

Can't or (No such word as Can't)

I can if you let me. At least I might.

Can I do it with all my might?
Oh can I please Hold your hand?
Whisper sweet something
Inaudible yet felt in your inner ear
Forget me knots that tie our tongues
Together?
Can't I please Kiss your toes, fingers, nose
Lips, taint, clitoris, nipples, knuckles
Knees, and your whole booty hole? Please can I:
     Scratch, tickle, smell, taste, lick, slurp, suck
     And catch the golden drops of sunshine on
The tip of my tongue like something almost remembered?
Can't I, please? I can if you let me. At least I might.
Oh can I for true, do this and more with you?
Will you let me have my way with you?
Entering you freely, easily, steadily, rhythmically,
Frequently in all entrances known
Perhaps yet undiscovered?
Visit your southernmost regions? Why can't I?
Hear you giggle, wiggle, moan, gasp, cry out, beg, plead,
jiggle and crave for even more?
Can I pretty please:

Do what I want when I want where I want with you whenever you want me to or no? Oh my, can I just: Justify it as inspiration for you to do that kinky thing that you never did before but have been waiting and wanting to do? Remind you that you have a great future behind you? Please can I get you on your knees? Keep your heart from boredom and your brain from contempt and your body from familiarity? Remind you that it is only kinky the first time? Forget about love and treat this like a one night stand every single time? Cannot I Be your Mr. Right Now and your Mr. Right? Can I do it with all my might? I can if you let me.

    At least I might.
    TONIGHT.

Scary Crazy

A human with nothing to prove
is a danger to himself and others.
Self actualization is the most dangerous station;
Don't let Maslow's limitations become ours.
Never stop checking to see if the shit
You're selling and we are smelling
Is still fertilizing the earth.

Acting Suggestions

Acting is not like riding a bike.
Best acting advice is
Don't act.
Breathe.

Sexologism

Having Sex is the
Same as
Connecting two
Space crafts together
So the travelers
Inside can
Hold hands.

More on morons

Oxy cottons to stupidity
While studying the
Deception of deceivers
Basket and vaccination
Weavers weave wonders for
Believers.
Who said PhD's and JD's
Are the only doctors
More desperate for
Authority than medical doctors?

Approaching Acting in 2025

Breathe.
Body= brain + heart + genitals.
Imagination.
Speaking: Just keep talking.
Thinking.
Style= Time + Pace.
Chakras make the invisible tangible.

Summer Hill Seven as Lord Summerhays and Gisela Chipe in Misalliance by G.B. Shaw. (circa 2006)

Actor top five list

Samuel L. Jackson.
Denzel Washington.
Laurence Fishbourne.
Jeffrey Wright.
Me.

Summer Hill Seven

Résumé

TopDog
A Soldier's Play
Platanos
Birth
Death of a Salesman
August Wilson
Arsht Center
Lincoln Center
Kennedy Center

Topdog|Underdog, play by Suzan-Lori Parks, directed by Walter Dallas, performed in theRoselle Center for the Arts (circa 2007) photo by Walter Dallas.

Summer Hill Seven

Original Kennedy Center Poemedy

Now. Romeo, don't know what he don't know Now!
Very Now and live is the winter of your discontent
Made glorious. Summer. This son of New York
And the clouds that lowered on this house.
Named for the slain POTUS take notice
And dig, dig, the irony of the two households
Both alike in Dignity in the fair DC once known Chocolate City,
Dig, dig the Ukrainian Romeo Romancing the Russian Juli and the
Palestinian rams tupping the Israeli Ewes
As the slain friend of the slain POTUS
Gave notice about the blue Black boy
Holding hands with the source of his own demise
Alike bewitchèd by the charm of looks,
Now is the winter of our discontent
Made glorious Summer by this son of York
Now is this Black ram tupping your white ewe
It's okay as long as the sheep are still light enough
Then the outsider sheep are still dark enough
Darker than the hue of a paper bag, baaaa
But boomp booomp baaaa, bump baaaat bump baaaat
Now Romeo is beloved and loves again,
But to his foe supposed he must complain,
Mumbling in the dark, drawing veils against the stars
Here now, in a house named for the slain and
Dark white sheep still steal love's sweet bait

AiR

From fearful hooks.
I know, You just wanted eggs,
On a toasted bun with turkey sausages
Instead you got an earful of Hamas and hostages
Being held a foe, you may not have accesses
To literature, history, knowledge
Because fear burns books
Look to breathe such vows as lovers use to swear
Here in white chocolate city where the green funding
Is listening with an artificial brain, to complain
They understand not a jot but they know, what Romeo
Don't know and that is even looking goes too far
And Juli, as much in love bewitchèd
By the charm of looks,
To meet her new belovèd anywhere even here in the
House named for the slain.
But passion lends them power,
Dig, dig....
Time means, to meet, mumble, mumble
Temp'ring extremities with extreme sweet.
Two households both alike?
Dig, assimilation, right Lorraine
The new Negroes ain't comfortable with
The new new Negroes and declare them rude
Rude am I, in my speech, nappy am I in my locks
Little blessed with the soft phrase of peace
Supercilious of me to embrace this chip of wood
You have placed upon my red shoulders
(Indigenous chant of woo woo woo)
Mumble, mumble, mumble in the dark
Babylon, crumble, crumble...
Look out Mr. President don't stumble

Summer Hill Seven

YOLO, we so close, though now is the time to
Make your Captain Kirk move.
Boldly go where no President has ever gone.
The full Monty. Mumble, mumble.

Temp'ring extremities with extreme sweet.
Let hands do what lips do and
Say it loud. We stand for ...peace.

Why!

If I kept doing
What I was doing
I'd never be doing
What I am doing.

SUGGESTED ACTIVITY 4:
Set your timer for 30 minutes and begin to inhale deeply and slowly exhale. Then after a few minutes of simply breathing begin to utter on each exhale a single verse line from one of the above poetic compositions. Continue this process until the 30 minutes have elapsed. Add this activity to your daily practice and record yourself to compare the growth in your ability to breathe out the sounds.

AiR

Black Men: From Da' Street to University & Back Again

FILM SCREENING and DISCUSSION WITH PRODUCER, DIRECTOR & Actors from the Cult Classic: **AS AN ACT OF PROTEST (2002)** by Dennis Leroy Kangalee

Dinner & Discussion with Founders of Stockton University's Chapter of Alpha Phi Alpha, PiXi and Actor Che Ayende

ΑΦΑ
ALPHA PHI ALPHA
FRATERNITY, INC.

WHEN? Friday, April 14, 2023, 7pm
WHERE? Alton Auditorium, Stockton-Galloway

SPONSORED BY OFFICE OF RESIDENTIAL LIFE

Artist-in-Residence
Summer Hill Seven
JD, NYU SCHOOL OF LAW |
MFA, UNIVERSITY OF DELAWARE

Essalogue V
Action and Movement yield Autonomy

"I practice hard, and when I play, I don't play what I practice. You can't think and play at the same time. When I play, I don't want to play the music; I want the music to play me."
- Sonny Rollins, American Tenor Saxophonist

AUTONOMY is a prerequisite to creativity. Your action and motion are evidence of your autonomy. Today I am acting like an acting coach to the stars. I have forgotten when I started coaching and teaching acting.

The promise of payment from a third party and the name recognition of the student makes this moment memorable. My action is moving and my movement speaks boldly.

My client today is exceedingly beautiful. Her honey complexion and naturally cascading cherry brown hair gives her the feeling of the quintessential girl next door. Her car, clothing, and charm immediately intimidate me.

She is careful to not be too friendly and I am appreciative of her kindness in popping the bubble in my imagination before it can fully inflate.

I am hired to prepare her for a role that I am intimately familiar with at a rate that is misunderstood by my employer. I won't discover the misunderstanding until after I send the invoice. I am new at the billing aspects of the "acting-coach" life.

My ambition is to avoid regular teaching and remain curious as an artist, yet at some point your own skill level becomes so excessive that the universe demands that you share.

My brief exchange with the client reveals that she has an undergraduate degree in theater and other professional credits. Now, she is primarily celebrated for being herself but I am not working with a novice actress.

I don't ask why she has chosen this role. The answer does not affect my work. She is beautiful. I don't want to linger in the presence of this woman who smells like sunshine on a spring day, therefore, I dive in directly to the text.

My approach to acting is entirely based on the text and/or movement of my character as defined by the text. I begin with addressing the movement because that is where I can begin to assess how this celebrity uses her breath.

Spearmint. Lilacs and spearmint. I continue to fall in love with my clients and some of my students, even now, several decades into my experience as an acting guru.

My entire approach to coaching and teaching, in fact, are about finding the apparent beauty that both I see and believe the client possesses and that the client also can see and believe and demonstrate how to apply that to every moment of their work.

I am led to believe that frequently, celebrities are insecure for a variety of reasons.

In this case Actress, her name for our purposes, is a mother and owner of many businesses earning at least a hundred times what I made last year. Nearly all my clients earn way more money than me, I would not have it any other way.

If you don't have money then you cannot handle nor relate to the truth about yourself as quickly. Poor people frequently suffer from denial about why they are poor.

Denial stands in the way of experiencing yourself truthfully. A truthful experience of our bodies is where movement for the actor lives. When an actor is unaware or more likely in denial about how she carries herself through space she is impossible to coach.

Acting is about nothing if it is not about being in touch with the levers of your sexuality. When you become exceedingly good at mastering your levers then, and only then, can you begin to learn how to work the levers of anyone else's sexuality.

Before working with Actress, I discovered Fay Simpson's exciting work in the **Lucid Body**. I continue my own "self-work" with her techniques and theories.

The beautiful woman in my personal life, at the time, who is also an extraordinary dancer, introduced me to this transformative work that looks at acting through the lenses of the 7 chakras. I don't bother Actress with such foolishness as technique or theory.

Coaching is, for better or worse, like acting itself, evidenced by the results.

Despite the beauty of Actress, I can also see in her grace evidence of an extensive dance background. You hope for dignity in your students because that speaks of an internal belief system but when you discover divinity you quickly become curious about your own karma.

In casting among actresses, it is a rare quality yet it stands out immediately.

Divinity is the quality of being like God. God is perfect without flaw. God is incapable of being wrong. How do we know that God is infallible? We know God is infallible because God has made that clear through action and word. God is incapable of expressing doubt.

The actor who hints at doubts about what to say or where to go does not measure up to the standard of divinity.

Actress has no doubts that as she moves through space the world delights in beholding her every movement as she delights in their delight as well.

When she speaks, she expresses no doubts about the rate of the words, the meaning of the words, the tone, shade and passionate humor in her text.

In this case, my work as the coach is very difficult. I have to say "something". No one is paying me my intentionally high rates to hear "that I don't have anything to say because the person they hired is divine and to make any adjustments is foolishness."

I start with Actress the same way I start with the poor slob who crawled out of the gutter. I tell her the truth. "You are perfect."

Yes, both the gutter snipe and the angel are perfect as they are because in a million years we will never find another on the planet to play them better than they are portraying themselves now.

If only all of our acting roles were who we already are then acting teachers and coaches would be able to finally retire and do something "else" with our lives.

Acting coaches exist to help divine creatures play gutter snipes and gutter snipes to portray divine creatures - both are formidable actor challenges. Both hood rats and princesses are composed of carbon, hydrogen, oxygen, nitrogen, and phosphorus.

Actress is coming to play a college student riddled with self-doubt, insecurities, flaws, and self-loathing. Actress is an adult mother who has made good decisions in her life that have led to this opportunity.

The character is a person who hopes to become like Actress. Actress must be led to the closet of her memory where her doubts are no doubt kept neatly in an oak file cabinet in alphabetical order.

My task is to transform the divine Actress before me into a puny sack of heaping hot shit so that the audience can witness her transformation. An audience can only sit in awe of her now.

The audience must be made to believe that on the inside and out of this goddess there is a curse of ugliness that is unbreakable.

I know the role we are working on together well enough to play it myself. I know what audiences feel is evidence of their own insecurity. I know that the way a person breathes in and how she exhales will reach an audience at a level that cannot be entirely evaluated by their mind.

We don't want the audience to think. We only want the audience's feelings. Hence we must leave feeling out of our conversation during preparation. We must only talk about mechanical matters and treat this aesthetically pleasing body like a series of pulleys and strings.

AiR

I dive right in with a request. I force myself to say something to make sure I have not lost the power of speech in front of the goddess: "Please give me the first paragraph of your big monologue". That is no help because every sound uttered by a divine creature is music.

"Perfect, please do the same thing again."

"Perfect, please do the same part again."

"Perfect, please do the same thing again."

Am I stalling? Yes and no. I learned from one of the greatest acting teachers I have ever encountered, Nina Murano, "Don't do or say anything until you have something to do or say."

"Perfect, please do the same thing again." After nearly ten repetitions of the first line, this time I add, "Please continue with the next sentence this time and give me both sentences." Just as I suspected, she is flawless. Now I am beginning to see my work here. It is not an assignment I like but it must be done.

Now the most important and dangerous question: "Are you ready to have some fun?" I have a peculiar sense of fun. Actress is fearless. "Yes." In my devilish mind, I hear "Take off all your clothes and run around the room".

I actually laughed aloud at myself and shook my head at me as I attempted to speak.

"Okay, now this time when you say the first sentence I want you to strike a pose at the beginning and end, then before you go on to the next sentence I want you to strike two different poses at the beginning and end of that sentence; does that make sense?"

Coaching is a particular type of acting where inside of your body you have an entire ensemble of all of your past encounters with acting—every acting role and every directing role becomes people who confer like a roomful of doctors conferring about a patient.

The discussions between my internal medical team frequently delves into the finer points of Stanislavski's Method, The Chekhov Acting Technique, Method Acting, Meisner Acting Technique, Shakespeare Acting Technique, Lucid Body Technique, Roy Hart Technique, Jewel Walker Technique, and Practical Aesthetics Acting Technique.

So whenever you give an instruction you must make certain the patient understands it because not each of the roles inside you understand it in the same way, nor do they language it in the same way, does that make sense?

"Yes." And Actress again is flawless. "How did that feel?"

"Fun."

"Perfect."

"Please do it again, but with all different poses, yes?"

"Yes."

Now, I am beginning to giggle because it is starting to feel like fun.

And I say what every actor must never forget and I want to marry a woman with a tattoo on her lower back of this, my primary coaching mantra: "the more fun you have the more fun your audience will have."

She does it again revealing secrets and hidden hurts through a rare display of silly vulnerability. I see her naked soul in every pose. I reward her kindness with: "that is truly beautiful, please go ahead and do that with every sentence in the monologue."

Then, we work our way through poses with the dialogue. I am not getting paid by the variety of approaches only by the results. I quickly found an approach that both the professional and the coach can equally embrace.

If it is not broken...continue to use it until it is broken. In this case, it did not break, but after we have gone through all the words that she speaks we still have plenty of time left so let's go deeper, "Shall we?"

We don't discuss it because it is beneath both of us, but we both know that we have found hundreds of new choices and actions for her to play. My goal is to introduce doubt into her life at the gut level without being detected by her mind.

An actor, especially a professional, understands that the job of the actor includes "never boring any audience". Now that she has heard my reaction to spontaneous choices she will "rethink" the choices every performance.

The mere act of reconsidering her choices, every time, will give her the same vibrational energy of doubt that is fundamental to the character.

In short, I tricked this divine creature into believing that she is a mere mortal by loving every choice. I loved choices that were so ridiculous that no sane professional would ever attempt.

The more ridiculous the pose, the more I loved it. Actress has lost all sense of how to entertain because she has been entertaining a foolish man who laughs at everything.

I only had the privilege of working this way with Actress because she was well trained, with a finely tuned instrument capable of producing sounds like an angel and floating like the wind.

In the remaining time, I will go right for the jugular now. I turn my attention to "air". In particular, the air that comes out of her throat when she is not speaking.

"Before we finish, do you want to play around with the sounds of the character a little bit?"

"Sounds like fun."

Actress begins to open up. I am surprised because this is her first response with more than one syllable. Let's start with your monologue and sing your last line five different ways. She is incapable of anything less than divinity, as she quickly belts out hooks from heaven.

"Perfect, same thing, five different ways."

This time the sounds are truly extraordinary.

"Perfect, same thing again, please."

"Now this time, do you remember when you did the sotto voce version? Add to that what you just did at the end of this version. Do you understand?" Finally, some doubt appears, and Actress says "I am not sure, can you repeat that please?"

"Of course, I'm not sure exactly what I mean but I think it might be fun if you started singing the last line sotto voce and then ended it with that big bold sound that you just did that last time you did it. Does that make sense?"

Actress confesses, "I'm not even sure what I just did...but let me give it a try."

Even now as I sit here reflecting on it, the memory brings tears to my eyes because no one could have contrived it but it was as magical a moment as any that I have ever experienced with another human.

I wondered for days after how that might have happened. Maybe I am a better coach than an actor, I thought. What had I actually done or said? Could I do it again? How would I know?

My self-congratulatory bubble was blasted by the third party who objected to my objectively high fee. They were quick to say we did not know that was a per hour rate "we thought it was the rate for all the sessions."

Well "We thought wrong, didn't we" is what I wanted to say but did not because it was the last time I would perform miracles before I received my money. Now I only perform miracles slightly bigger than the miracles I am paid to perform. Does that make sense?

SUGGESTED ACTIVITY 5:
Set your timer for 30 minutes and begin to inhale deeply and slowly exhale. Then after a few minutes of simply breathing begin to speak the lines of any of the poems in The Poetry chapter of this book. Repeat the exact same lines in at least 7 different ways until you settle on your top 3 approaches or choices for that same line. Finally record your top 3 choices for the chosen line for review in future rehearsals.

Essalogue VI
Personal Victories

"If you can think and not make thoughts your aim; If you can meet with Triumph and Disaster; And treat both those imposters just the same;"
- IF by Rudyard Kipling

Highly effective people, according to the research of Stephen Covey, focus on private victories and public victories are the result the world at large will experience. My failures are more effective teachers than my triumphs.

Being air also means that you are the Artist-in-Residence (AiR) over your own body. When you become an AiR actor then you are an Actor in Residence wherever you reside. The job of acting requires that you learn your lines and not bump into the future. I can tell you that the above job description of an actor given by Spencer Tracey, one of the stars of the Golden Age of Hollywood, is the minimum basic expectation or the lowest bar for the actor of today.

The requirements other than speaking the words as written and landing on your marks, occur in your imagination. The most popular acting advice that I came across before I began my training was to learn the 5W's. The five "w" words that an actor wants to answer about her character are: 1) who am I; 2) where am I; 3) why am I here; 4) what do I want; and 5) when do I want it. You may hear the questions articulated differently, yet, most actors I know begin their process by thinking and recording the answers to these five questions.

My process begins with me in the audience at my final performance experiencing the impact that I am hoping to have on the human witnesses. From this purely imagined experience, my imagination travels slowly back through the imagined experiences that led to the initial imagined experience until I finally arrive back in the present moment. The process of traveling on the superhighway of my imagination occupies nothing less than hundreds of real-time hours. I cannot tell you a number of hours that will make any sense because it is a very personal decision.

If you are very familiar with your character, it may take more travel time because you have more concerns given your awareness of the details. If you have no familiarity with the character, the imaginary journey in the beginning will be shorter because you don't know what you don't know and thus it will not occur to your imagination that there is a necessity to create an unknown.

Occasionally, your imagination will yield the unimaginable. Usually, the longer you use your imagination it will strengthen to the point of inventiveness. Invention is the abode of the pure artist. I only visit inventiveness at this stage of my development. I do not reside there for long because the contrast in the world draws me into conversations with the unknown. I have enjoyed the pleasure of working with pure artist and I promise that they exist in every variety of skin-bag: African, Gay, tall, fat, etc., and that each completed artistic project is the ladder upon which they have ascended to the pure place.

On the bottom of the artistic ladder is where we all begin. Even my son, who was born into and grew up immersed in an artistic environment, began without an imagination ladder. In the absence of an imagination ladder we crawl on the surface of the material world.

SUGGESTED ACTIVITY 6:

Set your timer for 30 minutes and begin to inhale deeply and slowly exhale. Then after a few minutes of simply breathing begin to imagine yourself receiving the highest award presently known for your chosen craft, i.e., Tony, Oscar, Emmy, etc., and just before you open your mouth to speak, stop and then imagine or perhaps create an imagination of each step in the process that led you to the podium where you are about to receive your award.

AiR

Seven with Theater Tallahassee Actor and Voice Actor, Ty Wold in a production of Frankenstein. Seven is The Creature and Ty Wold is Lacy, the blind man that befriends and teaches the creature how to utter human sound.(circa 2012).

Chapter Three: Of Art

You may shoot me with your words,
You may cut me with your eyes,
You may kill me with your hatefulness,
But still, like air, I'll rise.
- Still I Rise by Maya Angelou

Essalogue VII
Artistry

The Actor makes the moment and the audience makes the meaning.

The hallmark of a truly successful life is that you feel like a failure. As I walked around Lake Fred on the beautiful 1400 acre campus in the Pine Barrens of New Jersey, Stockton University, my alma mater, I enjoyed reflecting on my successful life as a failure.

Lake Fred was passing indifferent to anything I thought I had accomplished. She winked at me and whispered that she had lilly pads older than me. I giggled and strolled on reflecting on our earliest encounter in June of 1983. I was back home. As if by some miracle, I was walking around the same patch of earth 40 years later imagining another ladder. I was imagining being the scaffolding of a ladder upon which other artist will ascend and begin to develop an actual imagination ladder of their own to climb.

My process of acting begins with answers to basic questions about humanity at large and my character's relationship to humanity at large. Every character, dead or alive, has a relationship to air. Most of them breathe air. The characters that are dead do not visibly breathe yet the living actors that portray the dead actors must develop an approach to breathing that allows them to survive their performance of death. The relationship to air is the tangible evidence of your character's relationship to humanity.

Charles H. Fuller Jr. (left) was an American playwright, best known for his play A Soldier's Play for which he won the 1982 Pulitzer Prize for Drama pictured here discussing with Seven playwriting, casting, theatre, etc. at the home of Walter Dallas in Philadelphia, PA. (circa 2008) (Photo by Walter Dallas)

"Cromwell, however, treats the play as though it were carved entirely in air. The scenic design by Anna Fleischle allows only the barest minimum of set pieces to swoop in from above and sketch the various settings. Incorporating live music as a theatrical emollient, the staging risks turning "Death of a Salesman" into a funhouse with an array of expressionistic effects that only the great De Shields is able to stylishly pull off."

BY CHARLES MCNULTY
THEATER CRITIC |
Los Angeles Times
OCT. 9, 2022 6 PM PT

Seven (left), Steven Pelinski (center) as Willy Loman and Steve Hauck(right) as Ben, in Arthur Miller's Death of a Salesman. (circa 2008) "Perfect...everything you could ask of Miller's rich clssic" according to The Philadelphia Inquirer.

AiR

The audience makes the meaning and the actor makes the moment. During the pandemic of 2019 the citizens of America were as invisible as air. Our invisibility in fact led to a cleaner planet. The water was cleaner.

The earth was cleaner.

Most of all the air was cleaner.

Imagine, in being still, we allowed space to exist. Unoccupied space inside the earth's atmosphere is what I think of as air.

According to wikipedia, at the moment of this writing, the entry about COVID-19 begins with the following description of the pandemic of 2019:

> The COVID-19 pandemic, also known as the coronavirus pandemic, is an ongoing global pandemic of coronavirus disease 2019 (COVID-19) caused by severe acute respiratory syndrome coronavirus 2 (SARS-CoV-2). The novel virus was first identified from an outbreak in Wuhan, China, in December 2019.

Everything about the planet was transformed including and especially the art of acting, our subject in this book. I was teaching an artist residency with middle school students in Tallahassee FL at the behest of the Arts4All Florida program. Dr. Susan Baldino, my dear friend and colleague came for a sight visit on the day the news began circulating about masks and the deadly spread of the virus.

Normally, Susan and I would have hugged. Today we did not. Today, Susan wore a mask. Sometimes I pay attention to the daily news report but mostly I do not. I have found that news concerns me in the same way weather reports concern me.

Both reports are bits of information that allow me to dress myself, internally or externally, in a manner that lifts my spirits. I knew why Susan was distant. She may have even asked me if I had heard the news and I nodded continuing on with my work with the students.

When I returned home that afternoon, I received word that the residency was suspended indefinitely.

I was also engaged with another dear friend, the late Samuel Baba Olusegun Williams in a reading of the August Wilson cycle.

We had completed reading Gem of the Ocean, Joe Turner's Come and Gone and Ma Rainey's Black Bottom when the mask mandates and travel restrictions went into effect. Baba and I agreed that we can shift our meetings to a virtual location made possible by the Zoom corporation.

While Zoom was widely known before the pandemic, the stock rose sharply during the beginning of 2020 as more businesses felt compelled to turn to virtual meeting spaces to survive.

Baba and I continued working our way through the August Wilson cycle and we agreed that because of the pandemic, most of the great stage actors that we knew would be available to read these great plays.

We both, Baba and I, started reading Wilson's Pittsburgh Cycle with Gem of the Ocean and began reaching out and by the time we made it to Jitney, the seventh play in the cycle, nearly the entire cast was the same group of actors that I had the pleasure of working with in our live performance of the play in 2007 when I played Booster at the M Ensemble, in Miami Florida.

It was this Zoom reading of Jitney that convinced me we were at the dawn of a new form of acting in which we were creating the rules.

As I peeked my head up from my own work, I realized that the larger theatre community was also turning specifically to zoom to continue their work.

Baba and I continued to build our community by completing the reading of Radio Golf and then moved easily to A Raisin in the Sun and then we began to fumble along a bit.

My interest after Raisin was at first revisiting my earlier work in plays like TopDog, A Soldier's Play (which has not happened yet), and Death of a Salesman.

At the same time, I was refining and preparing to publish the Autobiography of Ray-Ray, a book of poetry. A friend and fellow thespian who I had not heard from in a decade or more, resurfaced in my life and invited me to attend a Zoom play-reading group.

The first night I went, I sat on the call without identifying myself—I wanted to watch without being watched. I wanted to watch to learn how other people were using this platform to create theatre art.

I also watched because my friend is an indigenous Black man and everyone on this Zoom call is some variety of Caucasian.

I become infatuated with the group after a 45 minute conversation with the Artistic Director, Johnny Clark, about humanity, art, public policy, theater, plays, Miami, Chicago and Zoom theater.

After that call, Johnny and I were bonded and we still have not met in person even after working together consistently for nearly two years. In fact, we were able to work together to create a zoom reading of Death of a Salesman with the following cast/crew:

WILLY LOMAN ....Tyler Wold;
LINDA .....Kim Hlavic;
BIFF .....Johnny Clark;
HAPPY ...George Alvarez;
BERNARD ...JaQuez Robinson;
THE WOMAN ...Sue Gisser;
CHARLEY ...AK Murtadha;
UNCLE BEN ...Summer Hill Seven;
HOWARD WAGNER ...John Kiyasu;
JENNY ...Sue Gisser;
STANLEY ...Jim Gleason;
MISS FORSYTHE ..Amy Marcs;
LETTA ...Cindy D'Andrea;
Waiter #2 & the Operator ...Cindy D'Andrea

Stage Directions... Sue Gisser and Amy Marcs
Directed by: Summer Hill Seven
Special Thanks: John Kiyasu

I was asked to share some "director's notes" and I stand by what I wrote even after witnessing the 4 hour recorded experience:

Thank you to everyone and everything that has allowed this series of moments to unfold. The genesis of this particular experience is unknown to me any longer. Yet what remains is a different way of thinking about Death of a Salesman.

Perhaps, I came into the process thinking that this experiment might be a curious way to examine the current conversation about race in post-Obama America. What I am leaving with is that Death of a Salesman is a curious way of examining my own inner life.

I now see my inner thoughts as a conversation between my own internal Willy, my Linda, my Biff, my Happy, etc., so that I am both entertained and enlightened by my own internal conflicts in a way different from when we began this journey.

I am humbled to create with and among you.

As of this writing the four-hour experience including the talkback after are all still available. Since I ended up filling in for Dennis Leroy Kangalee, who was engaged in creating **Krapp's Last Tape** for stage and film simultaneously, I did not have a chance to enjoy the reading live.

I do enjoy watching the tape.

Sue Gisser and I both experienced the frustrating joy of theater-making together while working on crafting the script for the reading. That is to put it in the language of this perspective I am sharing here, we were listening to the way the other human was inhaling and exhaling air.

In the empty space between our unique choices about breathing was created a refinement of the notes for breath for the actors to play with during the rehearsal process.

Air, again, is the truth, the whole truth, and nothing but the truth. It is fun to play with consonant and vowel energy, after all, that is what we do in theatre, isn't it? Yet we contend that such playing is ornamental to the substance of life which is the inhalation and exhalation of air.

We recommend beginning character work with exploring the breathing patterns of the character you are creating because that will give you a way of being when you are listening. Listening is what the refined actor must most master.

Listening while you are speaking; listening while your scene partners are speaking (not merely for your cue); listening when you are backstage; listening especially for the silence and the audience's response or lack thereof.

We recommend learning from listening to the air in the spaces and allowing your own breathing to be affected by what you have learned from the listening.

In many ways, like other teachers of acting, I describe it mimetically as a reflection of life, yet I know that isn't always true. Moreover, I am encouraging something more than mere mimicry in this approach that I am advocating for in our work together.

I am encouraging a rather objective relationship

with air in our work, that comes from an intentionality that we explore in our daily lives.

For many of us, who parade around with our artist flag at full mast all day, every-day, this may seem like an unreasonable ask. It may also be what your art is seeking to allow it greater freedom to soar and self-explore.

I am asking you to think of air first. I am asking you in effect to begin counting not from 1, but from 0.

We have talked, in other settings, about not memorizing words but rather becoming words. Now we are getting right down to it to say 'don't memorize breathing patterns for specific moments, be with the air of the moment that you are co-creating'.

In Johnny Clark's Vs. Studio on Zoom, immediately following our Death of a Salesman reading we enjoyed an evening described as "our inaugural Virtual Vs. Book Club night". The book is Isaac Butler's **The Method.**

I have not read the book yet, although Method acting is a fun subject and I can spend a lot of time listening and breathing in that conversation.

On November 15, 2022, I knew that I was completing this book about my own theories and ideas about the art of acting based on this concept of air. I listened to the air in this conversation with a great deal of specificity.

I wrote down some notes based on what I had heard, read and listened about Isaac Butler's book from other actors, magazine articles and the audio sample on Audible.

Two of these notes read:

"Your body of work is the tangible evidence of your technique."

"Acting is such a beautiful feeling that it is almost low-brow to talk about it."

Just before the discussion about Butler's book I enjoyed, for the first time, and immediately fell in love with the Michael Caine and Steve Martin film, Dirty Rotten Scoundrels.

I listened to the film as evidence of my own idea that the art of acting is the art of being air. Acting is breathing as air rather than merely a body taking air in and exhaling air.

This is a distinction that others may have, hopefully, described before and yet my independent discovery is corroborating evidence for such an approach. The Vs. Studio discussion was lively, enlivening, affirming and inspiring.

In fact, I like to give credit to this discussion for something I exclaimed that night which was "I have cracked my book" in the way that an investigator "cracks a case" or solves a mystery.

Creative writing is something far more mysterious to me than acting. The University of Delaware has given me the illusion that I am a master of the fine art of acting and please don't try to prove them wrong.

However, it has been many years since I have

been asked to "show and prove" my mastery, hence I have taken to the page to memorialize the accumulation of my thinking about the subject.

I listened to the air on the Zoom conversation about Mr. Butler's book and the passion was palpable; the experience was religious.

Johnny asked "what was Stanislavsky seeing that he said we need to approach acting differently" and I remember My Life in Art by Stanislavsky and his description of a particular performance of Othello that transformed how he saw the art form.

For me, I am not motivated to promulgate these ideas about acting because of any particular experience except perhaps the pandemic itself which is the genesis of this very Zoom conversation about Mr. Butler's book. The virus was deadly because it prevented its victims from breathing air. The pandemic was fear about whether or not humans can share and breathe air together.

Also it occurs to me in this Zoom conversation about acting that technique is like religion because we have plenty of atheists who do not believe in any approach.

Since "story" lends itself to heroes and villains, Mr. Butler's story about Method acting, as well as many I have heard before cast Lee Strasberg as the villain, practicing psychiatry without a license and Stella Adler as the Hero poetess, seeking the singular truth.

Like Dennis Leroy Kangalee stated in his inimitable way following a sublime production of Krapp's Last Tape in Brooklyn at Studio 111 on November 20, 2022 "I hate plot."

Yes, plot is mere contrived deception, while air is inevitably tangible—inescapable. A great actor must despise plot while still living truthfully despite it because even in the absence of it, the patient, i.e., audience member must create a plot.

Kangalee and his astute team of artists do everything in their power to give us some freedom from this iron ball of meaning-making that keeps us tethered to our suffering.

I felt it in the room, for what was an eternity of a few minutes where we existed in the empty space in Kangalee's Krapp.

We breathed together in an absolutely silent Brooklyn studio expecting what we knew not hoping for what we knew not in air that was alive. The air in the room breathed us into itself allowing us to breathe collectively for the first time again.

That is the new bar for our art. Acting that does anything less is no longer acceptable to me. I have priced myself out of the market while giving myself an infusion of capital to build all my artistic input on as we move onward and upward toward the fresh air in the light.

The audience makes the meaning, the actor makes the moment and never the twain meet. The untold secret of making a moment on-stage will be revealed to you when you decide to be air. Be Air. And breathe.

Acting Suggestions

Acting is not like riding a bike.
Best acting advice is
Don't act.
Breathe.

AiR

SUGGESTED ACTIVITY 7:
Set your timer for 30 minutes and begin to inhale deeply and slowly exhale. Then after a few minutes of simply breathing become the air you are breathing. Be Air. And Breathe.

Summer Hill Seven

BIRTH
a PLAY by Karen Brody
Directed by Summer Hill Seven

Eight Powerful & Hilarious Real-Life Birth Tales

Sept. 1 @ 7pm & Sept. 2 @ 2pm

To purchase tickets: (850) 597-9726
www.southsideartscomplex.org
click "SACTHEATER"
or visit
Southside Arts Complex, 2525 S. Monroe Street

Get in touch with your
Community.
www.TallyConnection.com

ImprovingBirth.org

My Last Will & Testament

Being of sound mind and body, the following is my last will and testament. I have one known heir. I bequeath all my worldly possessions to him. In the event other heirs are discovered, any further distribution will be at the discretion of my son, TRUETT XALIMON SUMMERHILL AKBAR.

The following testament will reveal the full extent of what remains from my life. My story is my only true possession. I will take it with me when I cease to exist.

To the extent that the residue of my story is of any value in the material world, then it belongs to my son. I am aware that my son may not find any value in it and he will have every right to refuse to take possession of any part of the bequeathal.

In such an event, the right of possession will fall to any of the adult heirs of my mother. The order of preference will follow their order of birth beginning with the oldest adult. The right of refusal shall begin with my siblings and pass to their heirs.

Provided that only one person may be entitled to complete possession at any one time.

My story begins with a dream that was formed before I was conceived. Yet it most certainly shall conclude with the final beat of my heart. My heart has been and at this moment remains my guide.

My heart stopped, I am told, when I was a toddler suffering from an infant hernia. I remember gaining consciousness and self-awareness on Sheridan St. in

Albany, NY. Pictures of me floating around my body existed in my mind's eye before I gained access to my body.

    I remember gaining control of my body in Head Start, a preschool program sponsored by the United States government. Emotions, internal feelings, and the like were not part of my experience until Kindergarten.

    Head Start was a location that I went to for food, language, exercise and to be "drilled in discipline and docility" as George Bernard Shaw describes it.

    In Head Start, we ate peanut butter sandwiches on white bread. We played "duck, duck, goose"—a game where children chase and run from one another. We were drilled on the sounds that the 26 letters of the English alphabet make.

    We were told when to take naps and rewarded with chocolate milk for our silence and compliance. I had no feelings about the experience or people. I remember nothing of the description of the people. I know only that the adult in the room was not my mother, father or grandmother.

    My emotional life began on my first day of Kindergarten and was expressed with violence toward my mother. My Dad, Bernard, was the man that I first distinguished as a man.

    I felt that whatever he was that was different from my mother, I was supposed to become, someday, such a creature. I was supposed to become a man. I knew primarily because I was chastised for being "too mannish" frequently by my mother whenever I spoke.

    I was being taught language while being chastised for using language. I was being hit by the hands of my mother for words that came from my mouth. After Head Start, I was taught to read words by my grandmother, Bernard's mother.

The words I learned were from studying religion with Jehovah's witnesses. My early vocabulary was a combination of words about God, Romper Room, Electric Company and all the words I could pick-up from the conversations that I heard my grandmother speak.

The sound of Lenore Van Hoesen, Bernard's mother, was the most easily recognizable.

My mother and dad took me to school # 24 in Albany, NY for my first day of Kindergarten and I felt as if they were leaving me there forever. I felt relieved because I would no longer be chastised for talking.

I snatched my hand from my mother and punched her in the stomach as I ran toward what I hoped was freedom.

I quickly realized that my mother's attempts to chastise me were preparation for what would follow from my ability to use language. I spoke the language of adults and that was a punishable offense.

The theme of my story is the punishment that has resulted from my use of language. Even until the very moment I cease to exist, I may continue to feel the pain of my own words. The above testament shall represent my last written words on the subject.

Cora's Conclusion

The answer to all of life's questions is that there is no answer to any of life's questions. You don't remember that yet. In this life, things happen and most people want to know why, when they eventually learn that something has happened. Most of the time people never learn that something happens.

When we found the white baby in our mailbox we wanted to know why somebody would put a baby in someone's mailbox. "It was God's plan" is the most simple and accurate answer for why. If you don't believe in the Grand Master of the Universe then you employ your faith in the pursuit of answers from other people. You often call those answers from other people, scientific. We were just about to contact the local sheriff about the white baby when my sister Charity came over with a message from my daughter Millie telling us that the little baby girl we found in the mailbox was born from Millie on February 24, 1935.

Millie did not tell us who the Father was and we came to know but we will not disclose that information. Why? Well, this is not a book about my family history, yet the family history of every artist is their greatest resource. You must continually create the unknown from the known. My great-grandson has created this book, with my help from knowledge and experiences that he does not have access to unless he employs the methods that he has shared with you in this book. He has only provided you with 8 essays written to be read aloud, that he calls essalogues from three distinct periods in his own life.

He has talked about his life before he was an artist, his life while studying art and his life after the formal study of the art of acting. This is relevant to your life if you want to become or understand art and artists. I have made him aware of questions and answers that he did not have access to before writing this book. Why? The nature of the art of theatre is based on faith in the unknown and is frequently described in the negative as the "willing suspension of disbelief". Seven finds a more powerful statement of this notion from his drama school coach Steve Tague who asked his students "Can you believe it more?"

That is what we want to leave you with, the idea that the more you believe in your art the more beautiful it will be in the world. We want to discourage you from focusing on explanations and justifications. We want to encourage you to do what Seven did with this book. He believes with all his heart that I am writing these words. He has never asked why I chose to finish writing this book. He is very grateful that I inserted myself when I did because he does not believe this book would exist unless I completed it. That is why, I made him aware of questions and answers that he did not have access to before he began writing the book.

Do not explain your art. Listen and see your art then unfold it to others. In the case of acting, the art involves you speaking from your mouth into your ears. Your ears must hold you accountable for the sounds from your mouth. The gestures or actions must speak for themself and the best you can do is practice stillness. In practicing the art of acting you must only move in ways that support the accountability and strict scrutiny of your ears. Utilize a mirror and visual recording technology to assess your gestures and actions yet rely on feelings.

Smile. That is the second acting tip that I want to

leave you with in this conclusion. Edith Skinner, author of **Speak with Distinction** reminds us that the sounds of the English language are more immediately available from the position of a smile. Again we refer you to Steve Tague who introduced Seven to the notion of a secret smile or smiling as if you have a secret. Any explanation of the secret smile lacks the power and depth of the practice of smiling as if you have a secret because you do have a secret. You have lots of secrets. Your secrets are what will make you a better actor. If you know you have secrets then you know that each secret has its own smile. AiR is a method or approach to acting and you now have access to this method that few will ever have. Use it wisely and responsibly.

Finally, my mother is Millie and my seventh child is Millie. My only living offspring are descended from my seventh child. My child Millie gave birth to the white baby in the mailbox that we gave a boy's name, Jimmy, named after my husband, her grandfather, James. Jimmy gave birth to ten children and the youngest is Ray-Ray or Seven, the author of this book and the man on the cover. Seven has one son, the baby on this cover, Truett. My father is Robert L. Summerhill. His father is William Summerhill. This book issues forth from all this history and an even more mysterious history. We have nothing else to say at this time. However, for the actors reading this book we encourage you to focus on your breathing of air. The practice of intentional breathing will bring you to the promised land of becoming air. My great-grandson has revealed the secret of the art of acting. Be one with the air. Be air. And breathe. Deal with the inhales and exhales and allow the language of the universe to regulate the remaining details.

Acknowledgements

This book began in my heart when I was a student at the Professional Theatre Training Program in Newark, DE, which was in residence at the University of Delaware. In my most challenging times I forced myself to think of reasons to press on despite feelings of fatigue, frustration or faithlessness. Sandy Robbins said it very simply to me when he told me "to tell yourself a big story or you will miss what there is here to get" and in that moment those words were familiar from another aspect of my life but I was not yet applying this approach to my daily life as a student of theatre. The most dangerous times in my life have occurred after achieving a dream or a victory beyond my expectations. My biggest dream, before the fall of 2004 was being able to attend a three year university graduate acting program that would lead to an MFA. Once, I achieved the dream, it was Sandy Robbins that reminded me to dream bigger. That is when this project began. This project became one aspect of my bigger dream.

I began actually writing this book after visiting Dr. Harvey Kesselman and he generously invited me to visit our alma mater in Galloway, NJ and to reside on campus while I wrote this book. Returning to Stockton University was another dream. Every dream come true gives birth to a series of dreams. One such dream was obtaining a Masters of Arts in American Studies from Stockton University. Dr. Thomas Kinsella was the first member of the faculty to offer to support the publication of this work. I am very grateful to Dr. Kinsella for publishing this work with the South Jersey Culture &

History Center and seeing that my story is included in a rich cultural and historical heritage in southern New Jersey.

Peter Murphy, the founder of Murphy Writing of Stockton University has profoundly impacted my writing. I am exceedingly grateful for his attention to my work and inspired by every opportunity to engage with his point of view about writing.

Dr. Steven Radwanski has made art a priority in the context of the residential life of students at Stockton University and I am inspired by his leadership. The theater faculty, David Reiser, Aaron Moss, and Dr. Venustiano Borromeo have warmly welcomed me and my artistic point of view. Professor John O'Hara and Dean Ian Marshall have been supportive of my scholastic endeavors at Stockton University as have many more people that I will fail to mention. I am very fortunate to be in this community of thinkers, readers, and educators.

Renee Tolliver patiently and without seeking any credit has supported this project especially during the final phase of getting the project across the finish line in a timely manner.

The images used in this book have a variety of sources and where we have not credited them, the source is unknown at the time of publication. In the early chapters we provide descriptions of the images. As the book progresses we leave the images to your imagination to create your own story. Your meaning is what matters most to you. As Leslie Reidel of the PTTP persuaded us, comprehension is merely the booby-prize in the appreciation of art.

Thank you to Vanessa Diaz, of AuthorHouse, and the entire production team. AuthorHouse has been a reliable partner in publishing all of my books.

Sharmin Islam Mannan's art has been a vital inspiration for completing this book.

Finally, as I prepare to publish my fifth book, it is still the lessons from the Kesselman dinner table which guide my sense of purpose. I know, because of those conversations, that it is worth it to continue to grow as a human not for my selfish gain or financial advantage, rather for the cause of advancing the human story.

Summer Hill Seven

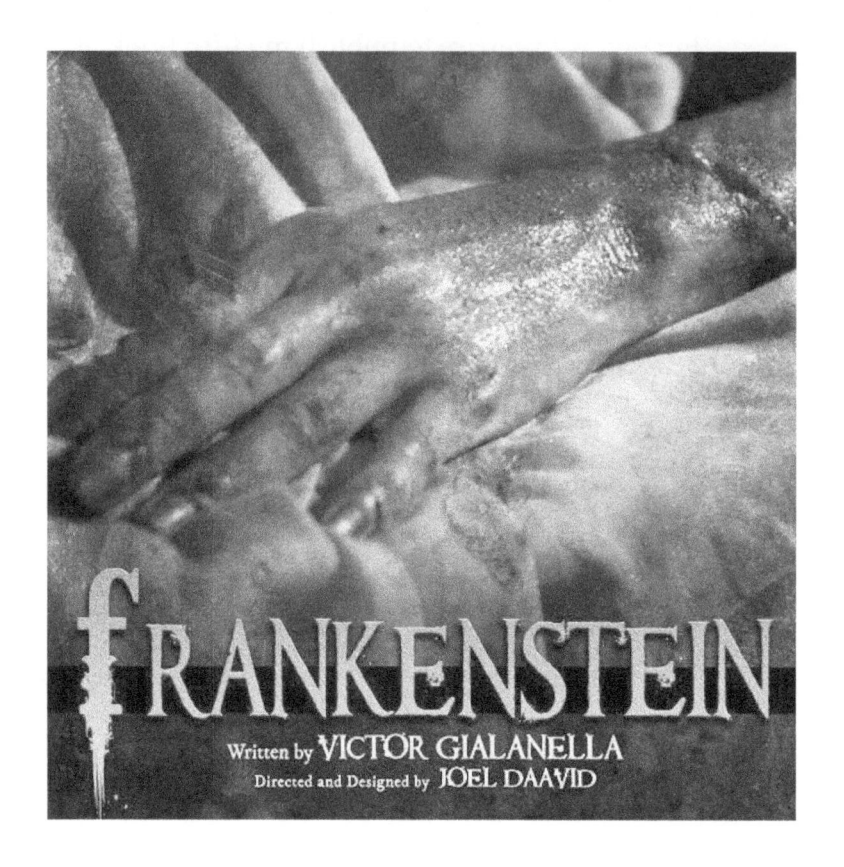

Annotated bibliography

Alex Preminger, editor of Princeton Encyclopedia of Poetry and Poetics (1965)

Amiri Baraka, previously known as LeRoi Jones and Imamu Amear Baraka, was an American writer of poetry, drama, fiction, essays and music criticism. He was the author of numerous books of poetry and taught at several universities, including the University at Buffalo and Stony Brook University. We met briefly at Stockton University when he was invited to speak in 1985. https://en.wikipedia.org/wiki/Amiri_Baraka

Arnold Rampersad and David Roessel with Christa Fratantoro, Selected Letters of Langston Hughes (2015)

Cary D. Wintz, editor of Harlem Speaks: A Living History of The Harlem Renaissance (2007)

David Troop, The Rap Attack: African jive to New York hip hop with Rap Photographs by Patricia Bates (1984)

Donna Akiba Sullivan Harper, Not So Simple The "Simple" Stories by Langston Hughes (1996)

Elijah Muhammad, The Theology of Time: The Secret of The Time (Messenger of Allah) edited by Nasir Makr Hakim (2002)

James Baldwin, Never Aired: Profile on James Baldwin ABC's 20/20, (1979) (https://vimeo.com/561405000)

Joel McIvor, Ice Cube: Attitude (2012)

Langston Hughes, The Big Sea (1940)

Langston Hughes, I Wonder As I Wander (1956)

Langston Hughes, The Best of Simple (1961)

Laurence Holder is an American playwright, poet, and director who focuses on the African-American experience. His plays often center historical African-American figures including Malcolm X, Elijah Muhammad, Thelonious Monk, Duke Ellington, Billie Holiday, and Zora Neale Hurston. We met when I began work as an adjunct professor at John Jay College in New York, shortly thereafter we began to collaborate on the work of Langston Hughes.
https://en.wikipedia.org/wiki/Laurence_Holder

Na'im Akbar, PhD, founder of Black Psychology, YouTube interviews.

Philip J. Deloria and Alexander I. Olson, American Studies: A User's Guide (2017)

Rakim (William Michael Griffin, Jr.), Sweat the Technique: Revelations on Creativity from the Lyrical Genius (2020)

Randall Kennedy, Nigger (2002)

Raymond Akbar, Summer Hill Seven, Squircular: An Actor's Tale (2010)

Raymond Akbar, Summer Hill Seven, Hang Time: A poetic memoir (2006)

Raymond Akbar, Summer Hill Seven, Notes of a Neurotic! Poet Tree: Essalogues, Plays & Poemedies! (2004)

Raymond Akbar, Summer HIll Seven, Autobiography of Ray-Ray & Other Ancient Ideas Like Hip-Hop (2022)

Raymond Akbar, Summer Hill Seven, The Summerhill7 Film (incomplete) (https://www.youtube.com/watch?v=O-NsbTRl09s) This is the remaining trailer of the film from which the term "poemedy" derives. (2003)

Raymond Akbar, Summer Hill Seven, Shelly Gaza and Matthew-Lee Erlbach remix the 18th Sonnet of William Shakespeare at the Utah Shakespearean Festival (2005) (https://youtu.be/zKCE4ha3gYo)

Raymond Akbar, Summer Hill Seven, Shakespeare N. Haarlem, The first act of the original solo performance of a play about a Puerto Rican Muslim spoken-word artist that is sentenced to death by lethal injection for a poem that he read at an open-mic in New Jersey (2002) (https://www.youtube.com/watch?v=Jj5vku12OTQ&t=1s)

Richard Pryor, Bicentennial Nigger (1976)

Richard Pryor portraying his original character Mudbone (2013)
https://youtu.be/VBCWgqLGHn4

Richard Pryor portraying his original character of Mudbone, The Warner Brothers Albums (1974 - 1983).
https://youtu.be/d6hwsx8xnPM

Richard Pryor, N****s, (2007) Concord Music Group, Inc., Wattstax - The Living Word

Scott Saul, Becoming Richard Pryor (2014)

Tupac Shakur, The Rose That Grew from Concrete, (1999)

William Jelani Cobb, NPR-wide series, **In Character**, is taking a long look at fictional characters and their significance in our lives. Today commentator William Jelani Cobb talks about "Mudbone," a character created by the late Richard Pryor. Cobb, a professor at Spelman College, is the author of To The Break of Dawn
https://www.npr.org/templates/story/story.php?storyId=17785153

William Shakespeare, The Tragedy of Othello, the Moor of Venice republished by W.W. Norton & Company, Inc. (2004)

About Poemedy

Eloquence is our business. Eloquence is fluent, persuasive speaking and writing. Summer Hill Seven is recognized as one of the foremost leaders in the conversation on creativity & eloquence in America.

He is a distinguished alumnus of Princeton University, New York University School of Law, University of Delaware's Professional Theatre Training Program, and Stockton University.

Karen Hunter, the Pulitzer Prize-winning journalist and New York Times bestselling author has described Summer Hill Seven as "truly one of the most important voices of our time."

You may schedule a private lesson, class, workshop, lecture or performance with Summer Hill Seven. You may also purchase our signature eloquence products including books, cd's, films and quality apparel. Each of our services and products reflect our complete love of all that is eloquent. Our methods deliver unique results in the following areas:

- Acting Lessons
- Personal Appearances
- Consulting Services
- Private Coaching
- Breathing Practices
- Public Speaking Lessons
- Creative Writing Lessons
- Creativity Therapy
- Movement Lessons
- Introduction to Salat

To learn more about Poemedy's one-on-one coaching, text "SPEAK" for an appointment now,
to 786-445-4918 or visit www.poemedy.com.

About the Author

Summer Hill Seven was born in Albany, NY in 1965 and given the name Raymond Bernard Larkins. He would change his name many times. He moved to Tallahassee, FL in 2012 and returned to Stockton University in January 2023, where he currently lives as an Artist-in-Residence.

Summer Hill Seven is the former president of the Big Bend Poets & Writers based in Tallahassee, FL. He is the author of the Poemedy Trilogy, a three volume work that introduces the particulars of the poetic form known as poemedy.

Two of his haikus are in the Voice of Trees Project, a public art installation, made possible in partnership with Italian artist Giovanna Iorio. The Voices of Trees Project is an effort to preserve the voices of poets and link their work to the landscape. Tallahassee and New York City, the only United States locations, join a global Voice of Trees community which includes Italy, France, England, New Zealand, Canada, Germany, Greenland, Ireland, Spain, Japan and the Netherlands. Both of these haikus are published in Autobiography of Ray-Ray & Other Ancient Ideas Like Hip-Hop.

He was the first Black president and first two-term president of the student senate at Stockton University, where he is an Honors graduate with a degree in political science and a certification in African-American studies in 1987 and is presently completing a Masters of Arts in American Studies. He graduated from the New York University School of Law with a Juris Doctorate. He graduated from the University of Delaware with a Masters of Fine Arts in Acting from the Professional Theatre Training Program (PTTP). He is an alumnus of Princeton University's school of Public Policy, State University of New York, Binghamton's Graduate Theatre program and the Rand Graduate School of Public Policy.

He graduated from elementary school at Philip Schuyler Elementary School in Albany, NY and High School at the Sister Clara Muhammad School in Philadelphia, PA.

He has performed at Lincoln Center, Kennedy Center, Arsht Center, Utah Shakespeare Festival, the Historic Asolo Theatre, Roselle Center for the Arts and many other venues.

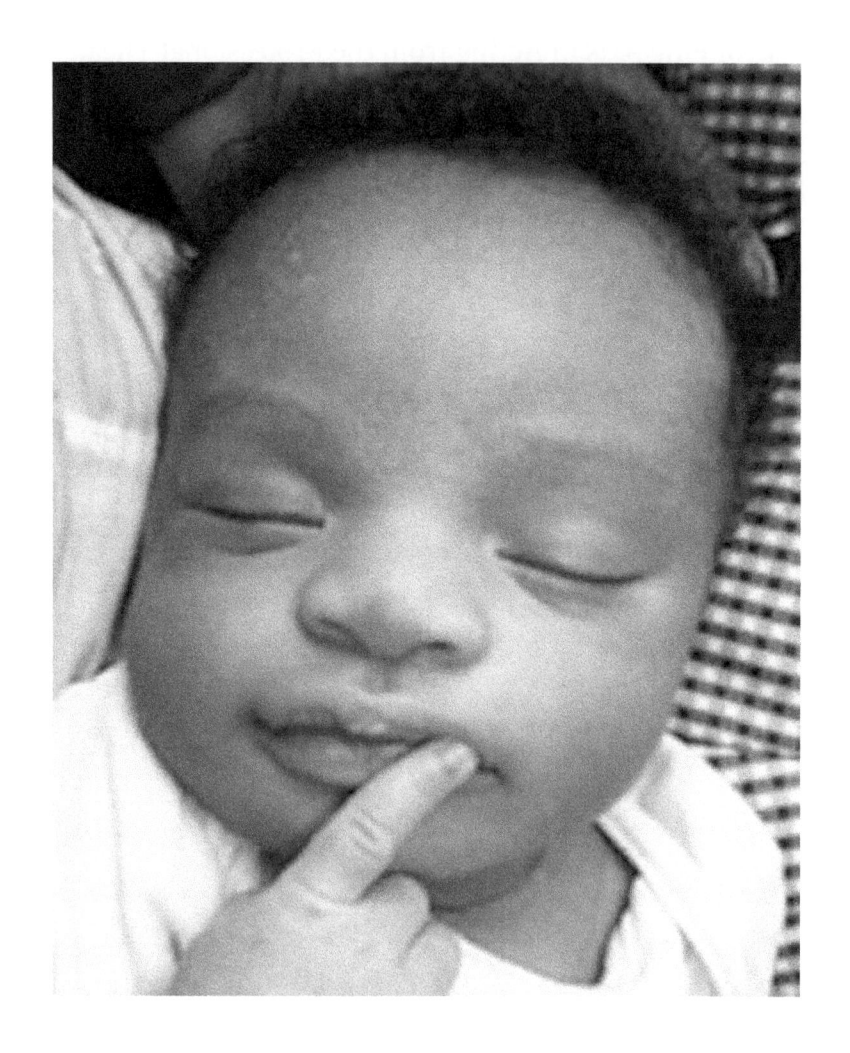

Summer Hill Seven

Praise for AiR

In a deeply compelling work of narrative art, Summer Hill Seven's AiR defies categorization. In part memoir, actor's study guide, and self-help book that reads as a novel, AiR offers a window into the inexplicable power of art—and especially the craft of acting. Mesmerizing, moving, and uplifting, Seven's story is at once Black, universal, unique, and always, always, deeply engaging. A must read for anyone interested in the art of performance — and the greater art of becoming a deeper, more lovingly engaged human being.

- Saladin Ambar,
Professor of Political Science,
Rutgers University,
author of Malcolm X at Oxford Union: Racial Politics in a Global Era

Praise for AiR

In AiR: The Poetry of Art, Summer Hill Seven writes a penetrating memoir as seen and felt through his eyes and breath and the "air" of his great grandmother, Cora.

A compelling series of essalogues details the twists and turns of the actor/poet who abandons his career as a lawyer for the love of art.

Accompanying the texts, meditative exercises and physical activities allow readers to associate and bond with the book's subjects and their theories.

Be inspired. Join one of our most talented artists-in-residence, Summer Hill Seven, to experience "angular" moments in a "squircular" world.

Susan Davis Baldino, PhD
arts advocate and professor of
Museum Studies,
Florida State University

Praise for AiR

Summer Hill Seven in his eloquent and elegant style weaves teachings and life lessons of artistic mastery through storytelling in his book AiR:
The Poetry of Art.

This book is the journey of a life long artist in residence (AiR); a skillful act organically designed with complexities and simplicity; requiring effort but also freedom like breathing.

Through the voice of his great grandmother Cora he shows us the interconnectedness of history and destiny, experienced in our past generations existing eternally through word, a thought, in Air.

As a student of Poemedy I am compelled to use its form to express my initial reaction to AiR… I can clearly see through my mentor and friend's story that with time "Life Is Always Perfected".

Thank you for your words Summer Hill Seven. Bless you as you continue to inspire culture across generations. Love. Peace.

Travis Xavier Brown
p.A.R.T. Productions
Artistic Director
Professor of Theatre
The George Washington University,
and Howard University

In loving memory of Walter Dallas, a giant of American Theater and former artistic director of the Freedom Theatre in Philadelphia. (September 15, 1946-May 3, 2020)